Texas Bucket List Adventure Guide

Explore 100 Offbeat Destinations You Must Visit!

John Mallon

Bridge Press
support@bridgepress.org

Please consider writing a review!
Just visit: purplelink.org/review

ISBN: 978-1-955149-43-3

FREE BONUS

Find Out 31 Incredible Places You Can Visit Next! Just Go to:

purplelink.org/travel

Table of Contents:

Corpus Christi

Crockett

Dallas

Del Rio

El Paso

How to Use This Book

Welcome to your very own adventure guide to exploring the many wonders of the state of Texas. Not only does this book lay out the most wonderful places to visit and sights to see in the vast state, but it also provides driving directions and GPS coordinates for Google Maps to make exploring that much easier.

Adventure Guide

Sorted by region, this guide offers over 100 amazing wonders found in Texas for you to see and explore. These can be visited in any order, and this book will help keep track of where you've been and where to look forward to going next. Each portion describes the area or place, what to look for, how to get there, and what you may need to bring along.

GPS Coordinates

As you can imagine, not all of the locations in this book have a physical address. Fortunately, some of our listed wonders are either located within a national park or reserve or are near a city, town, or place of business. For those that are not associated with a specific location, it is easiest to map it using GPS coordinates.

Luckily, Google has a system of codes that converts the coordinates into pin-drop locations that Google Maps is able to interpret and navigate.

Each adventure in this guide will include both the GPS coordinates and general directions on finding the location.

It is important that you are prepared for poor cell signals. It's a good practice to route your location and ensure that the directions are accessible offline. Depending on your device and the distance of some locations, you may need to travel with a backup battery source.

About Texas

Texas is the biggest state in the continental United States, second only to Alaska overall. It's located in the American Southwest and spans over 265,000 square miles. Twenty-nine million people call this state home. It features some of the nation's most notable cities, such as Houston, Dallas, El Paso, San Antonio, and Austin.

Texas became the twenty-eighth state on December 29, 1845. This was ten years after gaining its independence from Mexico. For that decade, Texas was its own nation, which is why you'll find a lot of Texas pride around the state. It's the only state in the country that was once a separate nation of its own.

Known as the *Lone Star State*, the state flag is the adopted flag of independence from Mexico. It symbolizes the independent spirit of Texans.

Texas is also known for its vibrant mix of cultures. Whether you're going for a stroll on San Antonio's Riverwalk or hiking the backwoods of Big Bend, Texas has a little bit of everything for everyone. In fact, Houston prides itself on being the most diverse city in the country.

Because Texas used to belong to Mexico, there is a strong presence of Mexican culture and tradition. Texans love to celebrate their rich cultural history, from statewide Día de los Muertos celebrations to family fajita BBQs on weekend afternoons.

It's also impossible to mention Texas without noting one of the state's treasures: Willie Nelson. Originally born in

Texas's Hill Country, Willie Nelson has been a mascot and advocate of all things Texas for the entirety of his career. He's a beloved figure in the great state.

Texas is home to beaches, swimming holes, mountains, deserts, swamplands, plains, and tropics. Its vastness is quite remarkable. The number of things to do in Texas is endless. There are museums and natural wonders all throughout the state as well.

A state that was once known for its oil and gas industry, Texas is now moving towards a bigger technology industry. People from around the country are moving to cities like Houston and Austin for the opportunities and excitement those regions offer.

Even though there's a lot of tech growth in the state, it still boasts plenty of open spaces. When driving through West Texas, you'll feel like you were plucked out of present-day life and thrown into an old Western film with its sprawling red mountains and tumbleweeds on dirt roads. Texas's natural landscape is as diverse as its people.

Landscape and Climate

Texas's landscape and climate are both wide-ranging. Its weather and natural scenery vary greatly from east to west and north to south. Texas is a huge state that covers a lot of land, boasting over 350 miles of shoreline along the Gulf of Mexico.

Folks from out of state tend to think of Texas as a dry, hot desert, but Texas is actually home to three different

4

types of climates. Each region has a unique landscape that contributes to the weather.

The northern panhandle is known as the "Texas High Plains." This area experiences extreme temperature ranges, low humidity, and little rainfall. It's known for its flat land, hot summers, and mild winters.

Central and coastal Texas is known for more humid weather, as it's closer to the Texas Gulf shoreline. It experiences colder winters and much hotter and more humid summers.

Finally, West Texas features the dry desert mountains that the state is known for.

Cadillac Ranch

Cadillac Ranch is one of the most intriguing art displays you'll find in Texas. It's located along the western end of Amarillo and features ten Cadillac cars that have been buried in the ground.

An art group buried the ten Cadillacs in 1974. The vehicles feature distinct tailfins that are still visible even with the front ends buried. The old Cadillacs have lost their original colors, thus encouraging people to add graffiti.

The art installation is one of the most prominent attractions on Historic Route 66. The famed route travels through Texas's panhandle.

Best Time to Visit: The spring and fall are good times, as the risk of excessive heat or snow is minimal.

Pass/Permit/Fees: Cadillac Ranch is free to visit.

Closest City or Town: Amarillo

How to Get There: From most major cities in Texas, take US-287 North off of I-45 or I-35W. The route goes through Wichita Falls and eventually into Amarillo. Head to I-40 West and take Exit 63. Look for the Second Amendment Cowboy statue near the gift shop.

GPS Coordinates: 35.18810 ° N, -101.98676 ° W

Did You Know? The cars here do get new coats of paint on occasion from private land operators, but it's mainly to create a new canvas for graffiti.

Palo Duro Canyon

If natural beauty that's millions of years old is your thing, then Palo Duro Canyon State Park is a must-visit in Texas. Perfect for day trips, overnight camping, or extended stays, this state park is located in the northern part of the Texas Panhandle. It's by far one of the most beautiful and scenic places to visit in that area.

The park was formed as a result of millions of years of erosion from the Red River and West Texas wind. It offers incredible views, scenic drives, picnic areas, historical sites, markets, and miles of hiking opportunities. And what would a Texas state park be without horseback riding?

Best Time to Visit: Spring or late fall. Summers in the canyon can get hot, so if you do visit at that time, it's best to go early in the morning.

Pass/Permit/Fees: Children under 12 are free. Adults are $8.

Closest City or Town: Amarillo

How to Get There: From the north: Head south on I-27 and east on TX-217. From the south: Head north on I-27 and east on TX-217. From the west: Head east on US-60 to TX-217. From the east: Head north on I-27 and east on TX-217.

GPS coordinates: 34.9373° N, -101.6589° W

Did you know? There is a descent of 800 feet to the canyon floor.

Six Flags Over Texas

Six Flags Over Texas has been entertaining thrill-seekers in Arlington since 1961. The park features more than forty rides over about 200 acres.

The theme park features some exciting roller coasters like the Titan, the New Texas Giant, Batman the Ride, and Shock Wave. There's also a carnival section with various family-friendly rides.

Six Flags Over Texas hosts live shows. Plus, you'll find plenty of restaurants and shops throughout the park. You can see the entire park from atop its oil derrick, which is about 300 feet high.

Best Time to Visit: The park is open year-round, but try going during the late part of the calendar year. You can visit the Fright Fest Halloween event in October and Holiday in the Park in November and December.

Pass/Permit/Fees: Tickets cost $79.99 at the gate, but you can buy them online for $39.99.

Closest City or Town: Arlington

How to Get There: The park is accessible via I-30 from both Dallas and Fort Worth. Take the Six Flags Drive exit to reach the park.

GPS Coordinates: 32.75770 ° N, -97.06731 ° W

Did You Know? The Titan is the tallest and fastest roller coaster in Texas. It reaches a height of 245 feet and can travel 85 miles per hour.

Blanton Museum of Art

The southern end of the University of Texas at Austin campus is home to the Blanton Museum of Art. The venue features a collection of more than 18,000 pieces. The museum focuses mainly on modern art from 1900 onward. It also includes a few hundred older European pieces, including works from Rubens and Vouet. There are also a few classical Etruscan and Greek vases on display here.

There is also a Latin art collection featuring works from Latinx artists. You'll also find a center highlighting prints and drawings from history. A few of these drawings come from Italian masters like Guercino and Raphael.

Best Time to Visit: Visit on Thursdays, as the museum offers free admission on that day.

Pass/Permit/Fees: Adult tickets for the museum are $12 each.

Closest City or Town: Austin

How to Get There: Take the Martin Luther King Boulevard exit on I-35 to reach the UT campus. Go west on the road, and you'll find the museum near Brazos Street. The Metro 18 and 640 bus routes also stop here.

GPS Coordinates: 30.28088 ° N, -97.73767 ° W

Did You Know? The outside of the museum features a glass-and-stone building donated by Ellsworth Kelly. The building is called "Austin" and features various square windows.

Bullock Texas State History Museum

The southern end of the University of Texas at the Austin campus keeps history alive through its Bullock Texas State History Museum. The museum highlights the history of Texas starting from more than ten thousand years ago. Various archaeological artifacts that were found in Texas are on display. The state's progress through the Texas Revolution and its annexation, Reconstruction, Depression, and Civil Rights eras are represented in the museum. You'll also find exhibits on how Texas has become a leader in the oil and gas field as well as technology.

Best Time to Visit: The museum is open year-round, but there are always unique exhibits lasting for a few months. Check with the museum for information.

Pass/Permit/Fees: Admission is $13 for adults, $11 for seniors, and $9 for kids.

Closest City or Town: Austin

How to Get There: The museum is across the street from the Blanton Museum of Art on the university campus. Take the I-35 exit to East Martin Luther King Jr. Boulevard and go west for a few blocks to Congress Avenue. Bus routes 18 and 640 can also take you to the museum.

GPS Coordinates: 30.28030 ° N, -97.73873 ° W

Did You Know? The museum also has a theater dedicated to showcasing performances from *Austin City Limits*, an Austin-based music performance show.

Hamilton Pool Preserve

Hamilton Pool Preserve is one of the most beautiful swimming holes in all of Texas. Its clear blue water and high grotto are summertime attractions for both Texans and out-of-state visitors. Thousands of years ago, the ceiling to an underground river caved in, resulting in intense erosion. After several thousand more years, the erosion eventually formed the beautiful natural pool we know today as Hamilton Pool Preserve. Take a short hike down to the grotto, and you'll see a majestic waterfall. There is a small shoreline beach for tanning and playing. Swimming is sometimes unavailable due to falling rocks, so please check the park site prior to going for a swim. The preserve itself has miles of trails to hike that will lead you out to the Pedernales River.

Best Time to Visit: Summer

Pass/Permit/Fees: Reservations are required for peak seasons. There is a fee for entry. For current prices and to book a reservation, please visit the park's page at: https://parks.traviscountytx.gov/parks/hamilton-pool-preserve

Closest City or Town: Austin

How to Get There: From the East: Drive west on US-71 towards Hamilton Pool Road. From the west: Drive east on US-71 towards Hamilton Pool Road.

GPS coordinates: 30.3424° N, -98.1269° W

Did you know? The preserve is home to the golden-cheeked warbler, a rare bird native to Texas.

Lady Bird Johnson Wildflower Center

The Lady Bird Johnson Wildflower Center is one of the beautiful attractions you'll find in southwest Austin. The center showcases more than 900 species of Texas-based plants. The hardscapes also have stones collected from throughout the region.

As the name implies, the Central Gardens are located at the heart of this destination. In addition to native flowers and plants, there's also an arboretum dedicated to various Texas trees.

The center is an ideal place for birdwatching, as estimates suggest that more than a hundred species can be found here.

Best Time to Visit: Spring is a good time to visit since reservations are not traditionally required during that season.

Pass/Permit/Fees: Tickets are $12 for adults and $10 for seniors.

Closest City or Town: Austin

How to Get There: Take the MoPac Expressway from downtown Austin, then take the La Crosse Avenue exit. Go south, then turn right to the center entrance.

GPS Coordinates: 30.18563 ° N, -97.87321 ° W

Did You Know? The facility uses a rainwater collection system to harvest the water necessary for maintaining the gardens. The center can store 68,500 gallons of water.

Lady Bird Lake

Lady Bird Lake flows through Austin and is the main attraction when traveling to the Texas capital. Although technically a reservoir, Lady Bird Lake offers 10 miles of surrounding trails with spectacular views of downtown Austin and its skyline. You can find many people hiking, biking, and gathering along the trail.

Originally created as a cooling spot for the downtown power plant, Lady Bird Lake has a surface area of 416 acres. The lake features many attractions such as boating, canoeing, paddle-boarding, evening cruises, bat-watching, and more.

Best Time to Visit: Spring or fall

Pass/Permit/Fees: No passes or permits are needed.

Closest City or Town: Austin

How to Get There:
From the north: Head south on I-35 to Riverside Drive.
From the south: Head north on I-35 to Riverside Drive.
From the east: Head west on US-290 to South Congress.
From the west: Head east on US-290 to South Congress.

GPS coordinates: 30.2477° N, -97.7181° W

Did you know? The South Congress Bridge that crosses over Lady Bird Lake is home to North America's largest Mexican free-tailed bat population.

Museum of the Weird

It's no surprise that a city like Austin—one that wants to keep things a bit unusual—would be home to the Museum of the Weird. This venue on 6th Street is dedicated to many oddities and curious things from around the world. It is inspired by turn-of-the-century dime museums.

You'll find many interesting artifacts at the museum, including bizarre animals, old movie monsters, suits of armor, shrunken heads, and wax statues. There's also a life-size model of King Kong on display there. The Fiji mermaid is one of the most intriguing exhibits at the museum. The mermaid is an artifact from old sideshows, where people would take the mummified remains of a fish and another object and sew them together.

Best Time to Visit: The museum is open throughout the year, but it is especially popular during the Halloween season.

Pass/Permit/Fees: Tickets are $12 each.

Closest City or Town: Austin

How to Get There: The museum is near Exit 234 on I-35. The museum is on 6th Street near the Jackalope, the Voodoo Room, and the Coyote Ugly Saloon.

GPS Coordinates: 30.26716 ° N, -97.73872 ° W

Did You Know? The museum has been featured on television programs like *Unsolved Mysteries* and *Mysteries at the Museum*.

National Museum of the Pacific War

The stories of the Pacific theater of combat during World War II come alive each day at the National Museum of the Pacific War. The museum is in Fredericksburg, the childhood home of Fleet Admiral Chester Nimitz.

There are exhibits on many aspects of the war. A hatch from the *USS Arizona*, a ship that was sunk during the attack on Pearl Harbor, is on display at the museum. You'll also see a B-25 bomber similar to what was used in America's first air attack on Japan in 1942. Other exhibits are dedicated to the battle at Iwo Jima, the development of the atomic bomb, and Nimitz's life and legacy. There's also a reenactment site where you can watch functioning tanks and a flamethrower in action.

Best Time to Visit: The museum is open year-round to the public.

Pass/Permit/Fees: Tickets are $18 for adults, $12 for military members with ID, and $8 for kids six and older.

Closest City or Town: Austin

How to Get There: The museum is about 80 miles west of Austin. Take US-290 West from Austin through Dripping Springs, Johnson City, and Stonewall to reach Fredericksburg. Turn right on Lincoln Street when you reach Fredericksburg.

GPS Coordinates: 30.27336 ° N, -98.86781 ° W

Did You Know? The Plaza of Presidents at the museum honors the ten presidents who served in the war.

The Texas State Capitol in Austin

The Texas State Capitol is the hub of local government operations. In addition to the Senate and House of Representatives chambers, the building includes many decorative elements worth seeing.

A terrazzo mosaic highlighting the six nations that governed Texas throughout its history is available for visitor viewing. There's also a distinct dome at the top that was loosely inspired by the United States Capitol. The rotunda features portraits of all the governors of Texas. Many monuments surround the building, including the Heroes of the Alamo Monument and the Pearl Harbor Monument.

Best Time to Visit: The capital is open to visit at any time of the year.

Pass/Permit/Fees: Tours are free and start at the north end of the capital.

Closest City or Town: Austin

How to Get There: The capitol is a five-minute walk from the Lavaca/12th, San Jacinto/12th, and San Jacinto/14th bus stops. You can take bus routes 1, 3, 7, 19, 20, 801, or 803 to get here.

GPS Coordinates: 30.27477 ° N, -97.74036 ° W

Did You Know? The dome is about 200 feet in height, making it one of the tallest in the world.

Beaumont Botanical Gardens

The Beaumont Botanical Gardens is one of the state's largest conservatories. They are located in the northern part of Tyrrell Park and are home to the Warren Loose Conservatory—a 10,000-square-foot building that highlights various plants from around the Americas. In addition to plants, you will find a serene waterlily pond swimming with goldfish and a long pool filled with koi. The gardens feature petrified wood spaces that hold plants that grew in ancient times. There is also an herb garden and separate gardens dedicated to camellias and agaves. Don't forget to visit the propagation house, which helps support the growth of new plants and the study of various species, including how well they can develop in Beaumont's distinct climate.

Best Time to Visit: Try visiting during the spring, as Beaumont is vulnerable to tropical systems in the summer.

Pass/Permit/Fees: The garden complex does not charge admission.

Closest City or Town: Beaumont

How to Get There: From Houston, take I-10 East to Exit 843 in Cheek. Take TX-124 East and turn on Parkview Drive.

GPS Coordinates: 30.02556 ° N, -94.14617 ° W

Did You Know? You'll find many pineapples around the center. The pineapple is a southern symbol of hospitality and comfort.

Boca Chica Beach

Boca Chica Beach is down at the southernmost point of the state in Brownsville. Recently, the beach has become notorious as the home of SpaceX, so traveling there can be tricky if not planned properly. Accessing the beach needs to be coordinated for times when it is open to the public.

Other than being home to SpaceX, Boca Chica Beach sits along the Gulf Shore and is known as America's "Third Coast." This beach is a semblance of where the United States ends and Mexico begins. Once a rapid river spilling into the Gulf, it's now a quaint and nearly untouched stretch of beach and nature.

Best Time to Visit: It's best to check when the beach is open to the public due to SpaceX activities.

Pass/Permit/Fees: There are no fees.

Closest City or Town: Brownsville

How to Get There: Take I-69 East towards TX-4 until you arrive at Boca Chica State Park.

GPS coordinates: 25.9965° N, -97.1501° W

Did you know? Although Texas beaches have many visitors each year, Boca Chica Beach only gets a few, making it a relaxing beach compared to neighboring ones.

Padre Island National Seashore

South Padre Island is known as the site of some of Texas's most beautiful beaches. It features swimming, restaurants, and nightlife, as well as extended stays on the island. Located at the southern tip of Texas, Padre Island National Seashore runs along the Gulf Coast and the Laguna Madre. Visiting this island is very much like stepping into the past because it is so well preserved. The shoreline does tend to get very crowded during the peak seasons and holidays, so be sure to plan your trip accordingly. There are a lot of outdoor activities, ranging from swimming to fishing and everything in between.

Best Time to Visit: For swimming, the best time to visit is summer. However, Padre Island National Seashore is open all year with plenty of activities.

Pass/Permit/Fees: Fees vary based on age, vehicle, and season.

Closest City or Town: South Padre Island

How to Get There: To reach South Padre Island, get on Highway 77 and drive approximately three hours south of Corpus Christi.

GPS coordinates: 27.4738° N, -97.2852° W

Did you know? Four countries have owned Padre Island at one point. In order, past owners include Spain, Mexico, Texas (when it was a country), and the United States.

Rio Grande Valley

The Rio Grande Valley rises above the Rio Grande River, which separates the United States from Mexico. The valley is home to a diverse blend of American and Mexican life.

Commonly known as simply "The Valley," this is the southernmost point in Texas. The subtropical climate allows for warm to hot temperatures all year long.

In addition to its beaches and sunny weather, there are also wildlife preserves and areas for watching butterflies, reptiles, birds, and small mammals along the seashore.

Best Time to Visit: The Rio Grande Valley features similar weather all year long, with hot temperatures peaking in the summer.

Pass/Permit/Fees: There are no passes or permits required to enjoy most of Rio Grande Valley, but there may be exceptions depending on which areas, parks, or reserves you visit.

Closest City or Town: Brownsville

How to Get There: Head south on US-77 towards Brownsville and South Padre Island.

GPS coordinates: 26.2034° N, -98.2300° W

Did you know? Each year, the Texas city of Brownsville and the Mexican city of Matamoros celebrate Charro Days, a three-day event promoting a vibrant, lasting relationship between two international cities.

Sea Turtle, Inc.

Sea Turtle, Inc. is an organization devoted to the rehabilitation of sea turtles. The venue in South Padre Island features a center where rescued sea turtles are treated for injuries caused by predators and water litter. Dozens of turtles are healed and re-released into the wild every year. While visiting, you'll also learn about these creature's importance within marine ecosystems, as these animals are critical for sustaining various habitats. This group not only provides vital rehabilitation care but works towards raising and breeding many endangered sea turtle species.

Best Time to Visit: The off-season from mid-August to May is a good time to visit.

Pass/Permit/Fees: Adult tickets are $10, while kids 17 and under cost $4. Seniors 62 and over, and military members with ID, cost $6.

Closest City or Town: Brownsville

How to Get There: You can reach the center by taking I-37 South to US 77 South, which becomes I-69 East in Harlingen. Take Exit 10B to TX-550, then go east on the Brownsville-Port Isabel Highway. Turn right on State Park Road 100, then go a few miles north on Padre Boulevard.

GPS Coordinates: 26.13780 ° N, -97.17249 ° W

Did You Know? The center is home to five resident sea turtles. One of these is Allison, the first sea turtle to have a functioning prosthesis.

Brazos Valley Museum Collective

You'll find the Brazos Valley Museum in the town of Bryan, not far from Texas A&M University campus. The museum features exhibits discussing Texas's natural history. Exhibits highlighting the evolution of life and culture throughout the state and collections devoted to geology, archeology, and the study of native mammals are on display. There are many fossils gathered from around the state, including the skeletons of a cave bear and a saber-toothed cat. There's also a section surrounding trail life and herding in Texas with a chuck wagon and various pieces of ranching equipment on display.

Best Time to Visit: The Booneville Days festival in October is a great time to visit.

Pass/Permit/Fees: Tickets are $5 each for adults or $4 for kids and seniors.

Closest City or Town: College Station

How to Get There: From downtown College Station, go north on Texas 6 Frontage Road and turn right on Briarcrest Drive to reach the Bryan Towne Center shopping complex. From Austin, go east on US-290. Head east again on TX-21, going right on the William Joel Bryan Parkway.

GPS Coordinates: 30.66745 ° N, -96.32084 ° W

Did You Know? The skeletal tail of a hadrosaurid is on display here. The dinosaur's tail is noteworthy in that it features fossilized skin.

Messina Hof Winery

The Messina Hof Winery in Bryan has offered some of Texas's most popular wines since 1977.

The winery is home to a vast vineyard which is available for viewing via tours. This showcases the lines of grapes, how they are harvested, and where they are fermented for the wines.

You can also try one of the winery's many vintages, which have won major awards in multiple international competitions.

Best Time to Visit: The Harvest Festival takes place every weekend in August and offers various get-togethers and tastings.

Pass/Permit/Fees: Tours are $28 and include tastings and food pairings.

Closest City or Town: College Station

How to Get There: From College Station, go north on Texas 6 Frontage Road, then right on Old Reliance Road. The road will go to the right, leading to the winery.

GPS Coordinates:
30.70248 ° N, -96.32327 ° W

Did You Know? The winery offers wines of all sorts, including reds, whites, dry wines, dessert wines, and sparkling wines. Many of these wines can be purchased at grocery stores and other retailers throughout the state.

Lake Conroe

Although it's named Lake Conroe, only a portion is located within city limits. The rest of the lake is in Montgomery County.

This 22,000-acre lake offers two swimming areas, fishing piers, playgrounds, and picnic spots along its coastline. It's a relatively quiet place to travel in Northeast Texas, and it's great for family camping activities and day trips.

In addition to the lake's amenities, you can also find activities and events like beach volleyball and horseshoe games for a friendly competition with your group.

Best Time to Visit:
The lake is open year-round, but the best time to visit for warm-weather activities is in late spring or summer, as they're only open seasonally.

Pass/Permit/Fees: There are no permits, passes, or fees, but you may need to pay for activities like boating and fishing.

Closest City or Town: Conroe

How to Get There: Follow US-290 East to W. Blue Bell Rd in Brenham. Take TX-105 East to FM 1097 East in Montgomery County.

GPS coordinates: 30.4369° N, -95.5985° W

Did you know? Lake Conroe was built as an alternate water source for Houston, Texas, in 1973.

Mustang Island

Mustang Island, home of Selena Quintanilla, is a small coastal town known for its Mexican culture. It offers a beautiful state park beach with sandy stretches for sunbathing, cool water for swimming, and plenty of campsites for visitors to enjoy on summer vacation.

Mustang Island State Park sits on the edge of Corpus Christi, just south of Port Aransas. The beach offers over five miles of shoreline and activities like fishing, swimming, surfing, and camping. If you're looking for a park to escape to in the summer, Mustang Island is a Texas must-see!

Best Time to Visit: Summer

Pass/Permit/Fees: Adults above the age of 13 are $5. Children under the age of 12 are free.

Closest City or Town: Corpus Christi

How to Get There: To reach the park, travel southeast from Corpus Christi on State Highway 358 to Padre Island, then cross the JFK Causeway. Continue one mile to the traffic light and turn left onto State Highway 361 (formerly Park Road 53). Go five miles north to park headquarters for a total distance of about 22 miles. The physical address of the park is 17047 State Highway 361.

GPS coordinates: 27.7104° N, -97.1629° W

Did you know? Mustang Island was named after the wild horses that once roamed the beach.

North Beach

North Beach is another Corpus Christi must-see stop along the Texas shoreline. This sunny Gulf Coast beach is home to some of Corpus Christi's most famous attractions. Visitors will find the Texas State Aquarium and the *USS Lexington*, a museum that was once an active aircraft carrier.

The beach offers tons of activities and amenities, including fishing, playgrounds, dining, museums, and more. There's really something for everyone in the family. A handful of beachfront hotels and resorts are available for enjoying extended stays along the coast.

Best Time to Visit: Summer is a great time to visit for swimming and water activities, but there are attractions and things to do all year long at North Beach.

Pass/Permit/Fees: There are no permits or fees to enter North Beach, but there are fees for various attractions.

Closest City or Town: Corpus Christi

How to Get There: Follow I-35 South and I-37 South to Seagull Blvd in Corpus Christi. Take the exit toward Texas State Aquarium/USS Lexington/North Beach from TX-35 North/US-181 North. Drive to Surfside Boulevard.

GPS coordinates: 27.8211° N, -97.3903° W

Did you know? North Beach consists of 1.5 miles of coastline along the Gulf of Mexico.

The USS Lexington

The *USS Lexington* served as an aircraft carrier in the Pacific theater of World War II and traveled through the Panama Canal to join the fleet. The carrier saw significant action in the Battle of Leyte Gulf and the Battle of the Philippine Sea. The ship was decommissioned in 1991 and today serves as a museum near the Harbor Bridge in Corpus Christi. Military aircraft are on display on the ship's deck. Visitors can also tour the bridge, the combat data center, and many other sites around the body. A flight museum, battle station simulators, and a 3D theater are available, allowing guests to experience the thrills of naval battles.

Best Time to Visit: The ship is open throughout the year, although the spring and fall are easier times to visit because the conditions are cooler.

Pass/Permit/Fees: Tickets are $18.95 for adults and $13.95 for children 12 and under. Military members can pay $14.95 when they present identification.

Closest City or Town: Corpus Christi

How to Get There: From San Antonio, take I-37 South and exit north to US-181 North. Take the exit to Timon Boulevard and turn right as you get to the road. Turn left on Breakwater Avenue, then left on Shoreline Boulevard.

GPS Coordinates: 27.81516 ° N, -97.38869 ° W

Did You Know? The *USS Lexington* takes its name from the Battle of Lexington, one of the first battles of the Revolutionary War.

Davy Crockett National Forest

The Davy Crockett National Forest is named after the Texas hero and contains more than 160,000 acres of woodlands, streams, trails, recreation areas, camping grounds, and wildlife habitats in East Texas.

This national forest is located in both Houston and Trinity counties within the Neches and Trinity river basins. President Franklin Roosevelt made this land a national forest in 1936.

Since then, families, hikers, and adventurers continue to visit the forest for its miles of hiking trails within the East Texas landscape.

Best Time to Visit: Spring is the perfect time to visit, though any mild temperatures and weather make for a great time in the forest.

Pass/Permit/Fees: There are a number of different types of recreation passes available.

Closest City or Town: Crockett

How to Get There: From the west: Head east on TX-7 through Kennard to Main Street.
From the east: Head west on TX-7 through Kennard to Main Street.

GPS coordinates: 31.2970° N, -95.1020° W

Did you know? Due to its location, there is a perfect blend of eastern and western birds that inhabit the forest. They're not seen together anywhere else in the state.

Dallas Arboretum

The Dallas Arboretum and Botanical Garden are on the eastern shore of White Rock Creek in northeastern Dallas. There are nineteen gardens spanning over 66 acres, including many showcasing plants from around the world.

The Color Garden provides a vibrant display, sprouting more than two thousand types of azaleas. The Red Maple Rill Garden has dozens of Japanese maples, while the Pecan Grove features about a hundred Japanese cherry trees. The arboretum is also home to a trial garden. The venue reviews how thousands of plants can handle the local climate and how well they can grow.

Best Time to Visit: The fall is the best time to visit, as the Pumpkin Village celebration includes thousands of pumpkins, gourds, and other seasonal plants.

Pass/Permit/Fees: It costs $17 for adults to enter and $12 for kids.

Closest City or Town: Dallas

How to Get There: Take the Winslow Avenue exit off I-30, then go north, merging right onto East Grand Avenue. Go north through Tenison Park and cross the southern end of the creek as the road becomes Garland Road. DART bus route 60 also stops near the gardens.

GPS Coordinates: 32.82144 ° N, -96.71655 ° W

Did You Know? There is a Spanish Colonial house called the DeGolyer House located within the arboretum.

Dallas World Aquarium

You'll find the Dallas World Aquarium in the West End District of downtown Dallas. The aquarium includes various habitats highlighting sea and rainforest animals.

There are ten tanks throughout the aquarium, with each highlighting aquatic life from many parts of the world. You'll find exhibits dedicated to fish and other mammals from Indonesia, Japan, the Bahamas, and Fiji. One aquarium features a tunnel that you can walk through to see the fish as they move.

There's also a rainforest habitat inspired by the Orinoco on the upper level. You'll see poison dart frogs, vampire bats, three-toed sloths, and many birds.

Best Time to Visit: The aquarium is open year-round, although it is not as busy on weekdays.

Pass/Permit/Fees: Adult tickets are $26.95, and kids' tickets are $18.95.

Closest City or Town: Dallas

How to Get There: Take the Woodall Rodgers Freeway off I-35 East in downtown Dallas and exit onto N. Griffin Street. The aquarium is to the right on Hord Street, a few blocks north of the West End DART light rail station.

GPS Coordinates: 32.78349 ° N, -96.80503 ° W

Did You Know? The aquarium features a few Xingu River rays. These rays are found in Brazil and are noticeable for their distinct dotted bodies.

Dallas Zoo

The Dallas Zoo brings the world of wildlife to southern Dallas. The zoo features more than four hundred species of animals, including a tiger habitat, a gorilla center, a penguin habitat, and a forest aviary. There's also a monorail ride here where you can see many African animals in their habitats, including the hippopotamus, the blue crane, and the Thomson's gazelle. Visitors can catch a glimpse of threatened and endangered creatures, including the African penguin, the great hornbill, the Puerto Rican crested toad, and the scimitar oryx. A primary focus is on the care and breeding of these unique animals.

Best Time to Visit: The zoo offers a concert series called Safari Nights on Saturdays in the summer. You can also visit on Dollar Day, which is held twice a year in July and November.

Pass/Permit/Fees: Ticket prices vary by season, with adults paying between $8 and $21. Kids cost between $3 and $16.

Closest City or Town: Dallas

How to Get There: Take Exit 425C for I-35 East from the north or Exit 425B from the south. The zoo is immediately to the south. You can also take the DART Red Line train to the Dallas Zoo station.

GPS Coordinates: 32.74094 ° N, -96.81294 ° W

Did You Know? The zoo features four lions, three cheetahs, and eight African elephants.

Denton Firefighters' Museum

The Denton Fire Department station on Hickory Street houses a museum dedicated to the firefighting field. The museum honors firefighters from the nineteenth century to the present day.

Visitors can see a hose cart from the nineteenth century, plus equipment from a 1935 truck. There are also old fire extinguishers and flame-retardant grenades, uniforms, helmets, and other items people have used for fighting fires over the years. The venue showcases the evolution of firefighting and how it has changed over time.

There is an exhibit dedicated to Denton firefighters who served in New York after the 2001 terror attacks. A 9/11 monument is located just outside the building.

Best Time to Visit: The museum doesn't host any special events, so you can visit anytime.

Pass/Permit/Fees: It is free to visit the museum.

Closest City or Town: Dallas

How to Get There: From downtown Dallas, go north on I-35 East and take Exit 464 to US-77. Turn right on Bell Avenue and look for the fire station to the left of Hickory Street.

GPS Coordinates: 33.21429 ° N, -97.12865 ° W

Did You Know? You can try on a firefighting uniform while at the museum. The uniform is rather heavy, as it is heavily padded and insulated.

Garland Landmark Museum at Heritage Crossing

The Garland Landmark Museum is located inside an old rail depot, displaying the history of Garland. Some of the exhibits showcase the city's railroads, the evolution of the city's arts scene, and a look at some of its old movie houses. Visitors can discover how Garland helped assist in managing various space exploration activities.

The museum houses a few old railroad cars. You'll see a 1910 Pullman Coach Car on display, although the inside part of the car isn't available to the public.

Best Time to Visit: The museum is open on Thursdays, Fridays, and Saturdays.

Pass/Permit/Fees: The museum is free to visit.

Closest City or Town: Dallas

How to Get There: From downtown Dallas, go east on I-30 and take Exit 56B to I-635. Go north and take Exit 11A to Saturn Road. Keep going north and turn right on Miller Road, then go left on Glenbrook Drive. The museum is also near the Downtown Garland stop on the DART Blue Line train.

GPS Coordinates: 32.91557 ° N, -96.63815 ° W

Did You Know? The museum building once served rail companies on the railroad tracks to the north.

George W. Bush Presidential Center

The George W. Bush Presidential Center honors the former Texas governor and United States president. The venue is on the campus of Southern Methodist University in Dallas.

Here visitors can find thousands of gifts and artifacts relating to Bush's presidency, including a full-size Oval Office replica.

The center also hosts the Native Texas Park, a space devoted to native Texas plants. When finished, dine at Café 43, which serves Texans-inspired foods with local ingredients.

Best Time to Visit: The center is open year-round and offers various special exhibits. Check with the center to see what's showing here.

Pass/Permit/Fees: It costs $26 to enter.

Closest City or Town: Dallas

How to Get There: From downtown Dallas, take US-75 North, then take a left on SMU Boulevard. Turn left on Bush Avenue to reach the center. You can also take the DART Blue, Orange, or Red lines to the SMU/Mockingbird station or use DART bus routes 521 or 768.

GPS Coordinates: 32.84127 ° N, -96.77819 ° W

Did You Know? A 22-foot steel bar from the original World Trade Center is on display here.

Grapevine Vintage Railroad

Take a ride on the Grapevine Vintage Railroad to see the many unique scenes around the Trinity River area via a vintage rail vehicle. The railroad cars are powered by a few steam locomotives and offer various special excursions throughout the year. You can take special train rides on many holidays, including Memorial Day, Easter, Mother's Day, and Father's Day. There's also a jazz-themed ride held each year in March, and separate Halloween rides for kids and adults every October.

Best Time to Visit: November and December are the best times to ride the railroad because of the North Pole Express train. The train offers a special Christmas-themed route featuring various attractions and shows.

Pass/Permit/Fees: Tickets cost between $18 and $26, depending on the cabin you use. The cost will also vary depending on different special events.

Closest City or Town: Dallas

How to Get There: From downtown Dallas or Fort Worth, take I-30 and then go north on TX-360. Turn left on S. Main Street to reach the station. The railroad is also near the Grapevine stop on the TEXRail Trinity Metro train route.

GPS Coordinates: 32.93386 ° N, -97.07799 ° W

Did You Know? The "Puffy" steam locomotive is one of the trains used here. Built-in 1896, it is one of the world's oldest trains in current use.

Heritage Farmstead Museum

The Heritage Farmstead Museum in Plano highlights pioneer life in a unique Victorian farmhouse built in 1891. There's also a second house nearby that you can see during your visit.

The museum houses hundreds of objects highlighting prairie life around the turn of the twentieth century. You'll learn about how people lived during that time and the many tools they used in running a farm.

The museum also features a one-room schoolhouse building. The building is a replica of an 1895 schoolhouse in Ponder.

Best Time to Visit: The farmstead is open year-round from Thursday through Saturday. It often has various temporary exhibits. Check with the museum to see what's happening here before you visit.

Pass/Permit/Fees: Tickets are $5 per person.

Closest City or Town: Dallas

How to Get There: From downtown Dallas, go north on US-75 and exit onto E. 15th Street. Go west, and you'll find the museum to the left slightly after crossing the Pittman Creek.

GPS Coordinates: 33.01909 ° N, -96.73100 ° W

Did You Know? You can enjoy a wagon ride on Fridays and Saturdays. The ride is included with your ticket.

Morton H. Meyerson Symphony Center

The Dallas Symphony Orchestra and various other organizations perform at the Morton H. Meyerson Symphony Center in the Dallas Arts District. This 2,000-seat venue features a unique structure designed by I.M. Pei. The Symphony Center hosts many classical music concerts throughout the year. These include events from the Symphony Orchestra, the Dallas Wind Symphony, and the Dallas Symphony Chorus. The inside of the center features a unique cylindrical arrangement. The ceiling is about 85 feet high, with 56 acoustical curtains to ensure the proper flow of sound throughout the building.

Best Time to Visit: Check the Symphony Center's calendar for information on events happening at the venue.

Pass/Permit/Fees: Ticket prices will vary for each event.

Closest City or Town: Dallas

How to Get There: The venue is in the northern end of downtown Dallas off Pearl Street near the Woodall Rodgers Freeway. The Olive at Ross and Flora stations on the M-Line DART light rail line are the closest mass transit stations to the symphony center.

GPS Coordinates: 32.78995 ° N, -96.79834 ° W

Did You Know? The center houses a massive pipe organ featuring more than 4,500 pipes. The organ is heavily inspired by concert organs of the nineteenth century.

Nasher Sculpture Center

The Nasher Sculpture Center features some of the world's most distinct sculptures on display, including those from artists like Matisse, Rodin, Picasso, de Kooning, Gauguin, Bertoia, and Duchamp-Villon. When finished inside, explore the outdoor garden on its northern end, which hosts many additional sculptures surrounded by various fountains and trees.

You'll find many traveling exhibitions and other programs at the sculpture center throughout the year. Past exhibits have focused on prominent sculpture artists like Melvin Edwards, Ernesto Neto, and Jaume Plensa.

Best Time to Visit: The evening hours are popular since the museum hosts social events with al fresco dining. Reservations are encouraged for these events.

Pass/Permit/Fees: It costs $10 to enter the center, although you can get a $2 discount if you present your DART card.

Closest City or Town: Dallas

How to Get There: The museum is south of the Olive at Flora M-Line DART light rail station. The venue is also accessible on Olive Street near the Woodall Rodgers Freeway.

GPS Coordinates: 32.78822 ° N, -96.80015 ° W

Did You Know? Some parts of the glass roof are covered due to concerns over reflective glare from the nearby Museum Tower.

Perot Museum of Nature and Science

You'll find the Perot Museum of Nature and Science in a massive cube building in Dallas's Victory Park neighborhood. The museum is dedicated to the study of the human body and the natural world.

Multiple permanent exhibit halls demonstrate how the body moves and how injuries occur. There's also a section that highlights Texas's three ecosystems, plus an area that shows how earthquakes and tornadoes are formed.

Explore exhibits dedicated to gems and minerals, energy development, and how life has evolved on the planet over billions of years. Many of these places include interactive activities for kids and adults to enjoy.

Best Time to Visit: The museum is open throughout the year.

Pass/Permit/Fees: Tickets to the museum are $20 for adults and $13 for kids.

Closest City or Town: Dallas

How to Get There: The museum is on Field Street near the Woodall Rodgers Freeway. The 29 and 183 DART bus routes will take you to the museum.

GPS Coordinates: 32.78707 ° N, -96.80658 ° W

Did You Know? The museum features a golden nugget mined in Australia that weighs more than sixty pounds. It is considered the world's third-largest golden nugget.

Reunion Tower

The Reunion Tower is the most noteworthy feature you'll find in Dallas's skyline. The tower has stood tall over the city's Reunion district since its construction in 1978.

Reunion Tower features a unique ball-shaped top that rises 561 feet above the city. You'll get a 360-degree view of downtown Dallas after you head up on a minute-long elevator ride. The building also includes a small outdoor observation area at the top.

Best Time to Visit: The evening is a great time to get a brilliant view of the sunset from the tower. You can also enjoy a beer or a glass of wine as part of the tower's Toasts on Top event.

Pass/Permit/Fees: It costs $18 for adults and $9 for children 12 and under.

Closest City or Town: Dallas

How to Get There: The Reunion Tower is across the light rail tracks from the Eddie Bernice Johnson Union Station. DART's Blue and Red lines and the Trinity Railway Express all have stations here. The Texas Eagle Amtrak train also stops at Union Station.

GPS Coordinates: 32.77569 ° N, -96.80886 ° W

Did You Know? The tower's globe features hundreds of LED lights that can change color to celebrate different occasions or events.

Texas State Fair

The State Fair of Texas lasts for 24 days each year, starting on the last Friday in September, and brings in more than two million visitors each year. The State Fair hosts an immense variety of activities, including concerts, a rodeo, a midway with games and rides, a wine garden, an auto show, and various shops highlighting products made in Texas. There are also creative arts programs and livestock exhibitions. It is particularly famous for hosting various food vendors that serve deep-fried foods. All this occurs under the watchful eye of Big Tex, the fair's mascot, a 55-foot statue with a massive cowboy hat.

Best Time to Visit: Thrifty Thursdays are the cheapest times to visit. The fair also offers various discounted food products on Thursdays.

Pass/Permit/Fees: Tickets cost between $15 and $20. It costs extra for food and tickets.

Closest City or Town: Dallas

How to Get There: Get on I-30, then take Exit 47 from the west or Exit 47C from the east. Fair Park station on the DART Green and Orange lines also serves the fairgrounds.

GPS Coordinates: 32.78210 ° N, -96.76579 ° W

Did You Know? The Cotton Bowl Stadium in the middle of the fairgrounds hosts two football games during the fair. These are the Texas-Oklahoma and Grambling State-Prairie View A&M games.

The Frontiers of Flight Museum

The Frontiers of Flight Museum is on the eastern end of the Dallas Love Field Airport. The Smithsonian-affiliated museum features various noteworthy aircraft on display, including a Learjet 24D business jet, the Meyer's Little Toot homemade biplane, and multiple Bell helicopters that were used for military purposes. The museum also has the original command module from the Apollo 7 space mission on display. You can see replicas of Sputnik 1, the 1903 Wright Flyer, and a Sopwith Pup. Other galleries include exhibits on the history of flight and the Love Field airport.

Best Time to Visit: Much of the museum is outdoors, so visit during the spring or fall season, if possible.

Pass/Permit/Fees: It costs $10 for adults to visit and $7 for kids.

Closest City or Town: Dallas

How to Get There: Take the Love Field exit on I-35 East to reach the airport. From the south, take W. Mockingbird Lane up to Lemmon Avenue. From the north, take W. Northwest Highway, then exit onto Lemmon Avenue. The Inwood/Love Field Green and Orange line DART station is the closest one to the museum, but it is two miles to the south.

GPS Coordinates: 32.84253 ° N, -96.83527 ° W

Did You Know? The museum features a few aircraft from Southwest Airlines, which is based out of Love Field.

The Sixth Floor Museum

The Sixth Floor Museum near Dealey Plaza in Dallas is located on the site where a sniper assassinated President John F. Kennedy in 1963. The museum looks at Kennedy's life, presidency, and his death in Dallas.

You'll see a full recreation of what parts of the building looked like on November 22, 1963, when the assassination took place. There are many artifacts related to the shooting, including various cameras from witnesses. The sniper's perch on the corner is also well preserved. The museum has an exhibit on the Warren Commission, the report that reviewed the circumstances of Kennedy's death. The FBI's full-scale model display of Kennedy's motorcade and the Dealey Plaza is featured here.

Best Time to Visit: The museum is open year-round.

Pass/Permit/Fees: It costs $18 for adults to enter and $14 for kids.

Closest City or Town: Dallas

How to Get There: Take the I-35 East exit to Commerce Street. Turn left on N. Market Street, then go left on Elm Street. The West End station on the DART light rail system is to the east.

GPS Coordinates: 32.77995 ° N, -96.80844 ° W

Did You Know? The Grassy Knoll where local clothier Abraham Zapruder shot the video of Kennedy's assassination is a short walk southwest of the museum.

White Rock Lake

White Rock Lake is a natural oasis away from the bustle of Dallas. Located in the northeastern end of Dallas, the White Rock Lake features 1,250 acres of space. The lake borders the Dallas Arboretum and Botanical Garden. You'll find the White Rock Dam on the southern end of the lake, which has provided the Dallas area with a full water supply since 1911. The lake offers a few boating ramps and piers for sailing. Kayak rentals are available for exploring on the water. There's also a bird-watching area run by the Audubon Society here.

Best Time to Visit: The spring season is an ideal time to visit, as the flowers and trees are in bloom, and the temperature isn't too hot.

Pass/Permit/Fees: It is free to visit White Rock Lake, but it will cost extra to rent one of the pavilions or kayaks here.

Closest City or Town: Dallas

How to Get There: From downtown Dallas, take I-30 East, then take Exit 49A to Winslow Avenue. Turn left on Winslow Avenue, then go right on Grand Avenue. Turn left on Winsted Drive to reach the southern parking lot. You can also go north on Lawther Drive to access the western parking lot.

GPS Coordinates: 32.82877 ° N, -96.72529 ° W

Did You Know? The lake features a 9.33-mile trail for hiking and biking.

Devils River State Natural Area

In a remote location in West Texas lies pristine, nearly untouched waters and virtually endless miles of hiking and biking trails. Devils River State Natural Area is a majestic place, but it does take some work to get there.

Devils River State Natural Area offers visitors a quiet, off-the-beaten-path place for catch-and-release fishing, hiking, biking, and primitive camping. This natural area tends to experience flash flooding, so it's best to travel during the dryer seasons.

Best Time to Visit: Spring or fall. Be sure to check weather conditions to avoid any flash flooding areas.

Pass/Permit/Fees: Adults 13 years or older are $5. Children under 12 are free.

Closest City or Town: Del Rio

How to Get There: From Del Rio, go north on State Highway 277 for 45 miles, turn left on Dolan Creek Road (gravel), and go 18.6 miles to the SNA boundary. Dolan Creek Road is a rough, 22-mile gravel/dirt county road with multiple low-water crossings. Use caution if you see flowing water! This is working ranch country, so please drive carefully and be mindful of loose livestock.

GPS coordinates: 29.939694° N, -100.970206° W

Did you know? Devils River State Natural Area has three ecosystems, making it a biologically diverse area.

Dolan Falls

Dolan Falls Preserve is fed by two popular and beautiful springs where West Texas meets the Hill Country. Devils River and Dolan Creek feed into this preserve, and locals boast that it is one of Texas's most pristine destinations to visit.

This nature preserve consists of 4,788 acres. In it, you'll experience the intersection of three distinct climates from the Edwards Plateau, Chihuahuan Desert, and the Rio Grande Plain. The combination of these terrains and habitats results in magnificent, unparalleled beauty.

Unfortunately, Dolan Falls is not open to the public. However, the neighboring Devils River State Natural Area is open year-round.

Best Time to Visit: The best time to visit is unknown as it doesn't accept public guests.

Pass/Permit/Fees: There are no passes, permits, or fees.

Closest City or Town: Del Rio

How to Get There: N/A

GPS coordinates: 29.8844° N, -100.9934° W

Did you know? The Nature Conservancy owns this land, and its main priority is to keep it preserved and protected. That's why public visitors are not allowed.

Seminole Canyon State Park

There's something truly magical about West Texas. It's the vision of Texas that folks around the United States imagine when they hear about the state. West Texas has tumbleweeds drifting on two-lane roads, desert mountains surrounded by blue skies, and places like Seminole Canyon State Park.

This park draws people in with its thousand-year-old pictographs from early Native Americans, but people stay for its beautiful scenery. The Rio Grande runs through the park, which separates the United States and Mexico. This southwest park is another treasure within Texas that's perfect for hiking and biking. It has 46 campsites, ranging from backwoods camping to full hookups with bathrooms on site.

Best Time to Visit: Spring or fall. It can be dangerous outside in the summer, so if you go at that time, make sure to go in the early mornings before the hottest time of day.

Pass/Permit/Fees: Adults 13 or older cost $4. Children under 12 are free.

Closest City or Town: Del Rio

How to Get There: The park is located nine miles west of Comstock on U.S. Highway 90, just east of the Pecos River Bridge.

GPS coordinates: 29.700094° N, -101.312875° W

Did you know? There are pictographs that are over 7,000 years old at Seminole.

Fort Davis National Historic Site

The Fort Davis National Historic Site in the western end of Texas is home to a well-preserved military fort that operated in the nineteenth century. There are a few dozen restored buildings showcasing many activities at the fort.

The site features about four miles of hiking trails. The trails include paths that led travelers to California during the Gold Rush. You can see panoramic views of the Davis Mountains from some of these trails.

Best Time to Visit: The park features historical reenactments during the summer months.

Pass/Permit/Fees: It costs $15 per vehicle to enter the site.

Closest City or Town: El Paso

How to Get There: From El Paso, take Exit 140A on I-10 East to U.S. Highway 90. Go south, then head east on TX-166 South. Take a left on Route 17 to reach the fort. From San Antonio, take Exit 209 for I-10 West and go south on Route 17.

GPS Coordinates: 30.60005 ° N, -103.89173 ° W

Did You Know? The park offers a scavenger hunt for kids, where they can find some unique natural features throughout the area. Kids who complete the hunt will receive special Junior Ranger badges for their work.

Guadalupe Mountains National Park

Guadalupe Mountains National Park is located in the large and vast Chihuahuan Desert of West Texas. It's home to the state's highest summit, Guadalupe Peak. From bloody battles between settlers and Apaches to the forming of a national park, Guadalupe Mountains National Park offers over 10,000 years of human history.

In the mountains, you'll find drawings from early Apache tribes. While historians and archeologists have studied the drawings, none have been able to interpret their meanings. Guadalupe Mountains is a beautiful park filled with a rich history.

Best Time to Visit: Year-round

Pass/Permit/Fees: $10 per person

Closest City or Town: El Paso

How to Get There: Guadalupe Mountains National Park is located in far West Texas on U.S. Highway 62/180. The driving distance is 110 miles east of El Paso, Texas; 56 miles southwest of Carlsbad, New Mexico; or 62 miles north of Van Horn on Highway 54.

GPS coordinates: 31.9231° N, -104.8645° W

Did you know? The Guadalupe Mountains were once underwater.

Hueco Tanks State Park

The Hueco Tanks State Park encompasses more than 800 acres of boulders and mountains slightly east of El Paso. The park is the perfect terrain for bouldering enthusiasts to climb and explore.

You'll find many pictographs drawn on the rocks throughout the park. These include paintings dating back as far as 6,000 BC. There are syenite pluton formations making up part of the Hueco Mountains. The area has been a spiritual site for many Native American tribes over the years, including the Pueblo, Hopi, and Kiowa people.

Best Time to Visit: October to March is ideal for a visit, as this is the traditional climbing season.

Pass/Permit/Fees: The park is free to visit, but you will need to check-in before visiting for bouldering, as some areas are off-limits for climbing.

Closest City or Town: El Paso

How to Get There: From El Paso, take I-10 East, then take Exit 24B to Buffalo Soldier Road. Turn right on Montana Avenue or U.S. Highway 62 East. Turn left on Hueco Tanks Road when you see the Flying Saucer Building.

GPS Coordinates: 31.91770 ° N, -106.04389 ° W

Did You Know? The park is surrounded by off-reservation trust land held by the Ysleta del Sur Pueblo people.

Davis Mountains State Park

There's no place more beautiful to stargaze at night than Davis Mountains State Park. Located high in the mountains in West Texas, this state park offers camping sites and miles of trails to hike.

Davis Mountains State Park is a great destination for those seeking a unique and remote experience. It's the right place for the more rugged adventurer. You can hike, backpack, mountain bike, go horseback riding, camp, stargaze, or study nature in all its glory. If camping isn't your thing, there is a lodge inside the park with full amenities as well.

Best Time to Visit: Spring or fall. If visiting in the summer, be cautious of the heat and UV rays.

Pass/Permit/Fees: Adults 13 years or older are $6. Children under 12 are free.

Closest City or Town: Fort Davis

How to Get There: Davis Mountain State Park is located one mile north of Fort Davis. It can be reached by taking Highway 17 to Highway 118 North. The park's road is the third entrance, about three miles down 118 North.

GPS coordinates: 30.5991° N, -103.9294° W

Did you know? This park was one of the first projects of the Texas Civilian Conservation Corps, a project started by FDR during the Great Depression.

McDonald Observatory

The western end of Texas, near Fort Davis, is home to the McDonald Observatory. The University of Texas at Austin operates the observatory on Mount Locke near the Davis Mountains State Park. There are four main telescopes for viewing and a fifth telescope available for visitor use. The most famous of which is the Hobby-Eberly monolith, a 10-meter telescope designed to survey the farthest reaches of the stars.

Best Time to Visit: The observatory is open for visits during the afternoon and evening hours. The evening is an ideal time, as the lack of light pollution in the area makes it easy for you to see the stars out here.

Pass/Permit/Fees: General admission is $3, while a guided tour costs $10. It also costs $25 to visit for an evening sky-viewing event.

Closest City or Town: Fort Davis

How to Get There: The observatory is about 400 miles west of Austin and 200 miles east of El Paso. From Austin, drive down I-10 and take Exit 209 to TX-17 South. The state route will go south to Fort Davis. From there, go west on TX-118 North. From El Paso, take I-10 to Exit 176, then take TX-118 South.

GPS Coordinates: 30.67302 ° N, -104.02216 ° W

Did You Know? The observatory is about 6,300 feet above sea level, making it one of the highest places to visit in Texas.

Clark Gardens Botanical Park

The Clark Gardens Botanical Park in Weatherford features an ever-changing landscape with a large variety of plants, flowers, and treas. The gardens feature a rose pavilion, an extended bowling green, an edible garden, an azalea grove, and a section blossoming with nearly four thousand iris varieties. Amongst the tranquil and scenic scape, a picturesque chapel is available for private events.

The Historic Tree Trail features trees from all corners of the world. Each tree has a unique historical significance. These include a clone of the weeping willow that shades Napoleon Bonaparte's grave. There are also trees representative of various presidents, literary figures, and other notable figures from American history at the park.

Best Time to Visit: The garden is open in the summer and winter by appointment only. It is open to the public without reservations in the spring and fall.

Pass/Permit/Fees: Tickets are $9 for adults and $5 for kids.

Closest City or Town: Fort Worth

How to Get There: From Fort Worth, take I-20 West to Exit 405. Turn right on the Ric Williamson Memorial Highway, then go west on US-180.

GPS Coordinates: 32.81207 ° N, -98.02307 ° W

Did You Know? You will find dozens of butterflies in the gardens. These include butterflies with orange, black, and white tones.

Dinosaur Valley State Park

The Southwest Fort Worth suburb of Glen Rose is home to the Dinosaur Valley State Park, a place where you can find preserved and fossilized dinosaur footprints. The park is in the middle of the Paluxy River and features more than 1,500 acres of land.

Fossilized dinosaur prints trek through the riverbed. These dinosaur tracks are near a few limestone deposits. Most of them are on the western end of the park near the water, but there's also a small spot in the east where they appear. About twenty miles of hiking trails and multiple campsites encircle Dinosaur Valley. Horseback riding and kayaking are available.

Best Time to Visit: Visit between April and October, as the park can freeze from November to March.

Pass/Permit/Fees: It costs $7 for adults to enter, while children 12 and under can enter for free. Horseback riding sessions and kayak rentals cost extra.

Closest City or Town: Fort Worth

How to Get There: From Fort Worth, take the Chisholm Trail Parkway south to Cleburne, then go west on US-67. Take Texas Route 205 West at the end.

GPS Coordinates: 32.24765 ° N, -97.81315 ° W

Did You Know? The entrance to the park features two life-size dinosaur models.

Fort Worth Botanic Garden

The Fort Worth Botanic Garden is at the western end of the city, to the north of the Fort Worth Zoo. Travel around the 1.75-mile loop path to see various gardens, including a rose garden and a garden dedicated to native plants. There's also a water conservation garden and another that is dedicated to pollinating plants.

The Botanical Research Institute of Texas is also at the garden site. The institute focuses on reviewing how plants grow and how they can propagate in various areas.

Best Time to Visit: The spring is the most popular time of the year to visit, as the flowers are in full bloom at this point.

Pass/Permit/Fees: Adult tickets cost $12, and kids' tickets are $6.

Closest City or Town: Fort Worth

How to Get There: Take the University Drive exit off of I-30 and head north. The garden is opposite Trinity Park.

GPS Coordinates: 32.74032 ° N, -97.36247 ° W

Did You Know? The cactus garden at the park is composed of unique soil, which includes crushed brick and granite. These features help preserve the water inside the soil to keep the cacti healthy even in the warmest conditions.

Fort Worth Zoo

The Fort Worth Zoo has supported the protection of exotic animals since 1909. You'll see many beautiful animals on display at the zoo, including penguins, primates, flamingos, cheetahs, meerkats, and elephants. The Museum of Living Art houses a reptile display with live king cobras, giant salamanders, and Burmese pythons.

The Texas Wild area highlights many animals native to Texas, including bobcats, horned lizards, and prairie dogs. This section showcases many animals from the state's mountain and desert areas. The Fort Worth Zoo also features a conservation program devoted to turtles. The group supports the reproduction of Asian freshwater turtles.

Best Time to Visit: The zoo has various holiday-themed events during the November and December months.

Pass/Permit/Fees: Adult tickets are $16, while tickets for kids 12 and under are $12.

Closest City or Town: Fort Worth

How to Get There: Take the University Drive exit off of I-30 and go south. Turn left on Colonial Parkway, then take a right on Flamingo Drive.

GPS Coordinates: 32.72339 ° N, -97.35647 ° W

Did You Know? You'll find three types of flamingos here at the zoo. The American flamingo has a more distinct pink tone than Chilean and lesser flamingos.

Fossil Rim Wildlife Center

You can drive your car through nearly ten miles of exotic animals in the Fossil Rim Wildlife Center in Glen Rose.

The center features more than fifty species of animals. These include a few endangered species like the Przewalski's horse and scimitar oryx.

Some of the animals here are unique to the state, including the blue wildebeest, the southern white rhinoceros, and the bongo. The wildlife center focuses on the conservation of these and many other animals.

Best Time to Visit: Since you'll drive your way through the center, there's no need to worry about the time of year for your visit. Some animals may not be as visible in the winter.

Pass/Permit/Fees: It costs $24.95 per car to enter the center.

Closest City or Town: Fort Worth

How to Get There: From Dallas or Fort Worth, head south to US-67 West. Go west through Cleburne and then turn left on TX 2008.

GPS Coordinates: 32.18356 ° N, -97.79598 ° W

Did You Know? The center has bred more than a hundred cheetahs since its formation in 1984.

Kimbell Art Museum

The unique worlds of European and Asian art are on full display at the Kimbell Art Museum in Fort Worth. The museum is housed in a Louis Kahn-designed building featuring distinct silver arches. There are more than 300 paintings on display, including works from Friedrich, Picasso, Monet, Cezanne, Matisse, Guercino, and El Greco, as well as an Asian collection featuring various sculptures and decorative pieces. Special exhibits visit throughout the year. Past exhibitions were dedicated to Nefertari-era Egypt, Renoir, Monet's later period, and Titian's *The Entombment of Christ*.

Best Time to Visit: The museum is open year-round, but check its website for details about special exhibits before you go.

Pass/Permit/Fees: It costs $18 for adults to enter or $16 for seniors or students. Children 11 and under can enter for $14.

Closest City or Town: Fort Worth

How to Get There: Take I-30 West from Fort Worth or Dallas and exit onto University Drive heading north. Turn left on Lancaster Avenue and then right on Van Cliburn Way.

GPS Coordinates: 32.74869 ° N, -97.36493 ° W

Did You Know? The museum is the only one in the Americas that houses a painting by Michelangelo. His earliest known painting, *The Torment of Saint Anthony*, is on display here.

The Fort Worth Stockyards

The Fort Worth Stockyards is a historic district in northern Fort Worth near Marine Creek. The stockyards are on land once used as a site for meatpacking and livestock auctions. Celebrating Fort Worth's western heritage, the district hosts cattle drives twice a day. You'll see plenty of longhorn cattle being brought out through the stockyard streets. After watching the cattle drives, you can shoot at a virtual gun range or tour the museum, which includes an exhibit dedicated to the life and legacy of John Wayne. There are also a few classic barbecue restaurants nearby.

Best Time to Visit: Visit on weekends as the stockyards host a fair that highlights how cattle herders work and the tools they use to herd their cattle. You can also see gunfight reenactments after the cattle drives on the weekends.

Pass/Permit/Fees: It is free to visit the stockyards, although each store and dining space has different charges.

Closest City or Town: Fort Worth

How to Get There: Take the NE 28th Street exit on I-35 West. Go left on N. Main Street, and you'll soon reach the stockyards.

GPS Coordinates: 32.78953 ° N, -97.34698 ° W

Did You Know? The stable on the stockyards grounds is one of the original stockyard buildings. It was constructed in 1912.

Bluebonnet Fields

Bluebonnet fields are scattered all throughout the Lone Star State. As the state flower, bluebonnets blossom in the spring and can be seen in parks and yards, along highways, and anywhere else wildflowers grow.

This purple flower with a blue hue resembles the shape of a traditional woman's bonnet, hence its name. Although there isn't a specific field to go visit, there are plenty of fields that bloom in the springtime. Many Texans take their Easter photos in a field of bluebonnets. They only bloom for a few weeks each year, so it's important to visit when they're in full bloom.

Some of the best areas for bluebonnets are the Willow City Loop or Wildseed Farms, which are along the Texas Hill Country region. These locations are also included in this book.

Best Time to Visit: Late March through May

Pass/Permit/Fees: None

Closest City or Town: N/A

How to Get There: N/A

GPS coordinates: N/A

Did you know? Texas Department of Transportation times its roadside mowing to allow for bluebonnets and other wildflowers to reseed for following years.

Enchanted Rock State Natural Area

As its name suggests, Enchanted Rock State Natural Area is a magnificent area filled with fascinating rock formations. This pink granite rock is close to the quaint town of Fredericksburg.

With its unparalleled beauty, the massive dome has attracted visitors for thousands of years. However, the dome isn't the only thing that's beautiful about Enchanted Rock. There are also many hiking trails, activities, and animal species to explore in the area.

Although swimming and biking are not allowed, you can try plenty of other activities like taking a long hike or stargazing in the open night sky. Enchanted Rock is a perfect nature-inspired getaway.

Best Time to Visit: Spring is the best time to visit. Nature is in bloom, and the Texas heat isn't as bad.

Pass/Permit/Fees: Entrance fees depend on peak seasons and visitor age.

Closest City or Town: Fredericksburg

How to Get There: The park is 18 miles north of Fredericksburg on Ranch Road 965. From Llano, take State Highway 16 for 14 miles south and then go west on Ranch Road 965.

GPS coordinates: 30.5066° N, -98.8189° W

Did you know? Humans have been camping in this area for over 12,000 years.

Wildseed Farms

Wildseed Farms in Fredericksburg facilitates the beautification and preservation of Texas through its springtime wildflowers. The farm's founder, John R. Thomas, knew the importance of wildflowers and the joy they bring to the public. He turned a small seeding business into a wildflower farm for folks to visit and to ensure flowers blossom and grow by Texas highways.

Along with breathtaking views of dozens of species of wildflowers, visitors to Wildseed Farms can also enjoy cold beverages and other refreshments. If you're traveling and want to bring a piece of the Texas Hill Country back with you, they also have a plant nursery and sell wildflower seeds.

Best Time to Visit: Wildflower season, which typically runs between March and October

Pass/Permit/Fees: This farm is open and free to the public.

Closest City or Town: Fredericksburg

How to Get There: Take Highway 290 in Fredericksburg to W/E Main St. The address is 100 Legacy Drive, Fredericksburg, TX 78624.

GPS coordinates: 30.2223° N, -98.7679° W

Did you know? The farm has over 200 acres of wildflower fields.

Willow City Loop

Willow City Loop is the most vibrant, scenic drive in all of Texas Hill Country. While it's a magnificent sight year-round, making the trip during wildflower season is sure to be the show-stopping beauty you're looking for.

Willow City Loop is located near Fredericksburg, a small, romantic town in the Texas Hill Country known for its peaches, wineries, and local shopping. If you're visiting Fredericksburg, planning a scenic drive through Willow City Loop is a must.

The small, two-lane ranch road twists and turns for thirteen miles through some of the oldest sites and habitats in Central Texas.

Best Time to Visit: Spring is the best time to visit, particularly during the wildflower season, which extends from late March to early May. It's also recommended to go on a weekday, as weekends can be quite busy.

Pass/Permit/Fees: There are no permits or fees.

Closest City or Town: Fredericksburg

How to Get There: Take 16 North (Llano Street) out of Fredericksburg. Proceed 13.3 miles, then turn right on RR1323. Continue 2.79 miles to Willow City. Turn left onto Willow City Loop.

GPS coordinates: 30.4005° N, -98.7008° W

Did you know? There are over ten types of wildflowers that bloom along the Willow City Loop.

Galveston Island Historic Pleasure Pier

Galveston Island features many fun sites straddling the Gulf of Mexico. The Galveston Island Historic Pleasure Pier is one of the most popular places to visit. The pier was built in 2012 on a complex where the original pier stood from 1943 to 1961. The old pier space has been refurbished and restored to its original glory. It stretches over 1,100 feet and has sixteen amusement rides, a 5D Theater, midway games, and a few restaurants, including Texas's first Bubba Gump Shrimp Co. location. There's also a candy shop at the pier.

Best Time to Visit: The pier is open year-round.

Pass/Permit/Fees: It's free to visit the Pleasure Pier, but it costs $26.99 for an all-day ride pass for adults and $19.99 for kids.

Closest City or Town: Galveston

How to Get There: From Houston, take I-45 South, then take Exit 1C to Harborside Drive to the east. Turn right on 25th Street, and you'll find the pier at the end of the road. You can also travel from Beaumont on I-10 West to TX-124 South and then Highway 87 South. You will require a ferry ride at Port Bolivar. After the ride, continue on Ferry Road and turn right on Seawall Boulevard.

GPS Coordinates: 29.39513 ° N, -94.78636 ° W

Did You Know? The Iron Shark rollercoaster at the park features four inversions and travels at 52 mph. It also takes you 100 feet up in the air.

Seawall Urban Park

Seawall Urban Park, located near Galveston Beach, marries the beauty of nature and the accessibility of urban living. Known for its summertime fun, it's a refreshing place to escape the oppressive Texas heat.

Seawall Urban Park offers visitors tons of activities. The urban park stretches along for ten miles and is home to the nation's longest and continuous sidewalk. This makes it a perfect place for running, biking, or taking a leisurely stroll with family and friends.

In addition to the summertime amenities along its coastline, there are also many beachfront restaurants, resorts, and attractions for tourists to the area.

Best Time to Visit: The most common time for visitors to tour Seawall Urban Park is the summer, but the park is open to the public year-round.

Pass/Permit/Fees: There are parking fees required to enter. You may not park or drive on the beach.

Closest City or Town: Galveston

How to Get There: Follow I-10 East and I-45 South to Broadway Avenue J in Galveston, then continue on Broadway Avenue J to Seawall Blvd.

GPS coordinates: 29.3015° N, -94.7739° W

Did you know? Seawall Urban Park is along Seawall Boulevard, which is central to Galveston's tourist attractions.

The Moody Gardens and Aquarium

The Moody Gardens and Aquarium in Galveston features three pyramids that showcase the beauty of nature. The first pyramid includes an aquarium with thousands of marine animals from around the world. The second pyramid is home to exotic rainforest animals from the Americas, Africa, and Asia. The third pyramid hosts unique traveling exhibits and a motion simulator ride film. During the summer, guests have access to a water park and a paddlewheel boat that offers day and night cruises along Galveston and a golf course lining the Syndor Bayou.

Best Time to Visit: November and December are great times to visit for the various holiday-themed programs.

Pass/Permit/Fees: A one-day, all-inclusive pass costs $60.

Closest City or Town: Galveston

How to Get There: From Houston, take I-45 South and exit on S. 61st Street. Go south, then take a right on Stewart Road a few blocks after crossing the water. The road soon becomes Jones Drive. Take a right on Hope Boulevard. You can also take State Highway 87 South if you're coming from Beaumont, but you'll require a ferry ride from Port Bolivar to Galveston.

GPS Coordinates: 29.27410 ° N, -94.85228 ° W

Did You Know? The rainforest pyramid features an extremely humid climate to simulate life in a rainforest environment.

The Ocean Star Offshore Drilling Rig and Museum

You'll find the Ocean Star Offshore Drilling Rig and Museum on the northern end of Galveston near the Galveston Channel. The museum exhibits a retired oil rig and various equipment that was used in actual offshore drilling. These include the pipe deck, the drill floor, and its transportation system. The rig includes exhibits on how people search for oil in the water and how it is produced and harvested. There's also a mock living space on board that highlights life on the rig.

Best Time to Visit: The museum is open year-round. Visit during the spring to reduce the risk of getting stuck in a tropical system.

Pass/Permit/Fees: Admission is $10 for adults, $8 for seniors and military members, and $6 for kids.

Closest City or Town: Galveston

How to Get There: Take I-45 South from Houston to Exit 1C, turning left on Harborside Drive. Continue for a few miles to reach the Strand Historic District. You can also reach the museum from Beaumont through TX-87 South, but a ferry ride from Port Bolivar to Galveston will be necessary.

GPS Coordinates: 29.31046 ° N, -94.79178 ° W

Did You Know? The Ocean Star was used along the Gulf Coast for nearly thirty years before it was retired and converted into a museum.

Inner Space Cavern

Inner Space Cavern is one of the best-preserved caves in Texas. It was discovered in 1963 by the Texas Highway Department, but it's estimated to be about 20–25 million years old. The cave runs more than 65 feet deep.

It's also one of the only caves in which preserved animal fossils from the prehistoric Ice Age were excavated.

The cavern is located in Georgetown, just north of Austin. It's a perfect location for summer fun. The Inner Space Caverns see thousands of visitors a year. There are many activities to do nearby. For more adventurous folks, you can even take the hidden passage tours. Whatever tour you take, the caves have magnificent views and discoveries for everyone.

Best Time to Visit: Winter, spring, or fall

Pass/Permit/Fees: Ticket fees depend on tours, groups, and age.

Closest City or Town: Georgetown

How to Get There: From the north:
Take Exit 259 on I-35 South toward Texas 26 Spur/Southeast Inner Loop.
From the south:
Take Exit 259 B on I-35 North toward SE Inner Loop Drive.

GPS coordinates: 30.6079° N, -97.6881° W

Did you know? The cavern was discovered after drilling through 40 feet of solid limestone.

Granbury City Beach Park

Granbury City Beach Park is a cozy stop southwest of Fort Worth. This small beach offers boardwalks, picnic tables, and sandy shores along Lake Granbury.

The City of Granbury is a historic town, and this park is one of its main attractions. Offering pleasant strolls along its boardwalk, swimming, a pavilion for outdoor activities, and kayaking, it's a must for families looking for a summer getaway in the northern part of the state.

While the park does not offer overnight camping, it is a perfect day-trip destination. The City of Granbury has a variety of hotels and bed and breakfasts for you to choose from if you'd like an extended stay in the area.

Best Time to Visit: Granbury City Beach Park is a great place to visit in the summer for its swimming and beach activities.

Pass/Permit/Fees: There are no passes or fees required.

Closest City or Town: Granbury

How to Get There: Take US-377 South to E. Pearl Street in Granbury.

GPS coordinates: 32.4418° N, -97.7813° W

Did you know? Lake Granbury is a man-made reservoir that was constructed in 1969.

Bayou Bend Collection and Gardens

Head to the western end of Houston to visit the Bayou Bend Collection and Gardens. The complex features a 1920s Neoclassical Revival mansion with a fourteen-acre garden. The property is the former home of local philanthropist Ima Hogg. The Bayou Bend Collection displays thousands of artistic items from the 15th to 19th centuries in more than twenty rooms throughout the mansion. The gardens include many pine and holly trees surrounding thousands of flowers. You'll find statues of the goddesses Diana, Euterpe, and Clio in some of these gardens.

Best Time to Visit: The mansion offers special holiday events in November and December. You can also visit the gardens during the spring season when the plants start blooming.

Pass/Permit/Fees: It costs $13 to enter the mansion and gardens.

Closest City or Town: Houston

How to Get There: From downtown Houston, go west on Allen Parkway near Exit 47 on I-45. Cross the Buffalo Bayou at Waugh Drive and then continue west on Memorial Drive.

GPS Coordinates: 29.76085 ° N, -95.42171 ° W

Did You Know? Most of the items here are from the United States, although there are a few European items that were brought into the country during its colonial period.

Delores Fenwick Nature Center

The southern Houston suburb of Pearland is home to the Delores Fenwick Nature Center. Take a stroll through the vast park area, located next to a freshwater aquarium with various native fish. You'll find about two miles of walking and running trails on the outside with access to a bat colony observation deck from the center.

The venue features a few interactive exhibits introducing unique wildlife found in Texas. There are some touchable tables featuring intriguing exhibits you can observe firsthand. There's also a craft table where people can produce various works of art based on nature.

Best Time to Visit: The center is open year-round and doesn't offer special events, so you can visit at any time.

Pass/Permit/Fees: The center is free to visit.

Closest City or Town: Houston

How to Get There: From downtown Houston, take I-45 South and exit on the Sam Houston Tollway. Go west on the tollway, then exit south on Telephone Road. Turn right on Magnolia Parkway.

GPS Coordinates: 29.54581 ° N, -95.30875 ° W

Did You Know? There are a few rookeries at the center that highlight various native birds from around the area.

Holocaust Museum Houston

The Holocaust Museum Houston hosts exhibits on various resistance efforts during the Holocaust, including the 1943 prisoner uprising in Warsaw. The building also has a railcar that was used to transport Jewish prisoners and a Danish fishing boat that was used to move Jewish people to neutral sites.

The venue stresses the search for social justice and how it continues to this day. You'll find displays surrounding genocides recognized by the United Nations and how people have been combating them over the years.

Best Time to Visit: The museum hosts various exhibits during the year, so check the schedule to see what is open.

Pass/Permit/Fees: It costs $19 to enter the museum.

Closest City or Town: Houston

How to Get There: Take the Main Street exit off of I-69 and go south. Turn left on Wichita Street, then turn right on Caroline Street. The museum is also near the Museum District stop on the Metro Red Line.

GPS Coordinates: 29.72549 ° N, -95.38573 ° W

Did You Know? The Butterfly Loft sculpture at the museum features 1,500 butteries, with each representing a thousand children who died in the Holocaust.

Houston's Museum District

The odds are you'll find a museum that interests you while in the Museum District in Houston's downtown sector, which is home to more than 150 museums.

The Houston Zoo takes up much of the district. The zoo is to the south and features an Asian elephant habitat and an African forest habitat. Some of the museums you'll find here include the Children's Museum Houston, the Houston Museum of Natural Science, the Houston Museum of African American Culture, and the Holocaust Museum Houston.

Best Time to Visit: The museums are open throughout the year, although the spring and fall are more temperate times for visiting.

Pass/Permit/Fees: Admission costs will vary by museum.

Closest City or Town: Houston

How to Get There: The museum is directly north of the Texas Medical Center and east of Rice University. Take the Red METRO light rail line to reach the district. The Wheeler, Museum District, Hermann Park/Rice University, and Memorial Hermann Hospital/Houston Zoo stations stop in the district.

GPS Coordinates: 29.72066 ° N, -95.38532 ° W

Did You Know? There's a full-size golf course in the southern end of the district. The Hermann Park Golf Course is open to the public.

Museum of Fine Arts Houston

The Museum of Fine Arts Houston is in the city's museum district. You'll find one of the country's largest art collections here, with works representing six continents. The museum displays nearly 70,000 works. You'll find art from Van Gogh, Cezanne, Monet, Rembrandt, Botticelli, and Cranach, the Elder, at the museum. The collections include works from various Texas-based artists, including many of Latinx and African descent. There is also a complete collection of Persian art.

Best Time to Visit: Check with the museum to see what exhibits are open. The museum often has multiple exhibitions running throughout the year.

Pass/Permit/Fees: Admission is $19 for adults, $12 for children ages 13 to 18, and free for children 12 and under. Military members also receive free admission when they provide their ID. General admission is free on Thursdays, but some exhibitions still require separate tickets.

Closest City or Town: Houston

How to Get There: The Museum District stop on the METRO's Red light rail line is one block to the east of the museum.

GPS Coordinates: 29.72603 ° N, -95.39055 ° W

Did You Know? Make sure to check out the in-house cinema which plays foreign films.

NASA Johnson Space Center

Many of America's greatest space travel triumphs were manned at the NASA Johnson Space Center in Houston. With about 250,000 square feet of exhibits and nearly 400 artifacts, you'll discover the amazing history of space travel at the Smithsonian-affiliated museum on 1601 NASA Parkway in southeast Houston. You'll see a full-size replica of the Space Shuttle outdoors at Independence Plaza atop Shuttle Carrier Aircraft 905.

The Mercury 9 and Gemini 5 capsules are on display, as well as the Apollo 17 module. Many spacesuits used throughout history, including the one Pete Conrad wore during his moonwalk on Apollo 12, are located within the exhibits.

Best Time to Visit: The museum is open throughout the year. Check its website to see what exhibits are open and when they will be there.

Pass/Permit/Fees: Tickets are $29.95 for adults and $24.95 for kids ages four to 11.

Closest City or Town: Houston

How to Get There: From downtown Houston, take I-45 South to Exit 24. Go left on the NASA Bypass, then turn left on Second Street.

GPS Coordinates: 29.55212 ° N, -95.09806 ° W

Did You Know? The center features one of only eight moon rocks in the world that people can actually touch.

Rothko Chapel

The Rothko Chapel is a place of unity in the Houston area. The chapel is a non-denominational house of worship where all cultures and religions are welcome.

The Rothko Chapel features a distinct New Formalist design. The interior includes a skylight that borders the building's irregular octagon shape. The inside also features fourteen paintings from abstract painter Mark Rothko.

Best Time to Visit: The chapel is open every day of the week except Monday. It is open throughout the year, but there are some private worship events that occur here on occasion.

Pass/Permit/Fees: It is free to visit the chapel.

Closest City or Town: Houston

How to Get There: The chapel is at the western end of downtown Houston. You can take Exit 127 off of I-69 and then go west on Alabama Street. Turn left on Yuppon Street to reach the chapel. The chapel is across the street from the University of St. Thomas campus.

GPS Coordinates: 29.73775 ° N, -95.39617 ° W

Did You Know? The *Broken Obelisk* sculpture by Barnett Newman stands outside the chapel. It was dedicated to Martin Luther King Jr. shortly after his death and transported to Houston as a gift.

San Jacinto Monument

The San Jacinto Monument has a design similar to the Washington Monument, but the San Jacinto Monument is slightly taller. At about 567 feet, it is the world's tallest masonry column. The San Jacinto Monument is an octagonal column made with reinforced concrete and Texas limestone. It features a massive star at the top, while the bottom reads an inscription on the formation of Texas. You can visit the top of the San Jacinto Monument in the Houston suburb of La Porte. You'll see the battleground of the Battle of San Jacinto from the top. The adjacent museum is filled with artifacts regarding the battle that resulted in Texas's independence from Mexico.

Best Time to Visit: Visit the monument during the morning before outside groups start to reach the space. The monument isn't as busy in the morning.

Pass/Permit/Fees: Adults can reach the top of the monument for $10, while children cost $5 each.

Closest City or Town: Houston

How to Get There: From downtown Houston, take I-45 South to I-610 East, then exit onto Texas Highway 225 East. Take a left on Independence Parkway, then go right on Vista Road.

GPS Coordinates: 29.75246 ° N, -95.08064 ° W

Did You Know? Look for the six flags of Texas while entering the monument. The flags honor the six countries that have had control over Texas throughout its history.

Jamaica Beach

Jamaica Beach is located in Galveston County along Texas's Gulf Shore. It's a small beach city with welcoming shore vibes that make it a quaint summer getaway.

If you're not a fan of popular tourist spots, Jamaica Beach is the city for you. Unlike bigger attractions along the Gulf Shore, like South Padre Island and Port Aransas, Jamaica Beach attracts a much calmer crowd.

According to the 2010 census, the population of Jamaica Beach is only 983 people. So, if you plan on an extended stay in the area, you may just become a local yourself!

Best Time to Visit: Spring or summer for warm-weather activities like swimming, kayaking, and camping

Pass/Permit/Fees: Jamaica Beach doesn't require a pass to visit the town, but there may be fees for entrance to certain attractions and beaches in the city.

Closest City or Town: Jamaica Beach

How to Get There:
Follow I-10 East to TX-342 Sput South/Broadway Street in Galveston. Take exit 1A from 1-45 South.

GPS coordinates: 29.1897° N, -94.9796° W

Did you know? Before becoming a town, Jamaica Beach was a burial ground for the Karankawa people.

Pedernales State Park

A state park filled with limestone, rivers, and relaxation lies just thirty miles west of Austin. Pedernales State Park is located in Johnson City and offers visitors opportunities for camping, hiking, and other outdoor adventures.

Swimming in the Pedernales River during the hot summer months can be a refreshing and relaxing break from everyday life. There is adventure available around the park with its miles of hiking and mountain biking trails. You can even plan a stop at a nearby Texas gem, the Hamilton Pool Preserve.

Best Time to Visit: Summer is the best time to visit for swimming if the river has enough water. Otherwise, it's beautiful all year round.

Pass/Permit/Fees: Adults 13 years and older have a $6 entrance fee. Children under 12 are free.

Closest City or Town: Johnson City

How to Get There: The park may be reached by traveling nine miles east of Johnson City on FM 2766 or by traveling west from Austin for 32 miles on U.S. Highway 290, then north on FM 3232 for six miles.

GPS coordinates: 30.3081° N, -98.2577° W

Did you know? The park was privately owned until the state of Texas bought it in 1970.

Caddo Lake State Park

Texas has a diverse landscape. From desert to tropics, it contains a wide range of wildlife, climates, and habitats. Caddo Lake Park is known for its piney landscape and is one of the few natural lakes in the state.

Located in East Texas, Caddo Lake is surrounded by a mossy canopy created by the cypress trees sprawling out of the water. This state treasure is a great place for canoeing and fishing.

You're welcome to camp, hike, look for a geocache or boat in the park. There are historic cabins for rent for the less-experienced camper, or there are 46 different campsites ranging from full hookups to water-only sites for the more rugged types.

Best Time to Visit: Year-round

Pass/Permit/Fees: Adult fees are $4. Children under 12 are free.

Closest City or Town: Karnack

How to Get There: Travel north of Karnack one mile on State Highway 43 to FM 2198. Go east for 0.5 miles to Park Road 2. The park is 15 miles northeast of Marshall.

GPS coordinates: 32.680233° N, -94.1790764° W

Did you know? Caddo Indians were the original settlers of the land in the 18th or 19th centuries.

Kemah Boardwalk

On the eastern end of Clear Lake in the town of Kemah near League City, the Kemah Boardwalk offers over fifteen rides, including the Boardwalk Bullet roller coaster, to keep the whole family entertained. Take a ride into the Galveston Bay on the Boardwalk Beast. The ride is a fun thrill, but be prepared to get wet. You'll find various shops at the boardwalk, including a gift shop and a candy store. There are also many restaurants here, such as Landry's Seafood House and Bubba Gump Shrimp Co. locations.

Best Time to Visit: The boardwalk is open year-round, but it is especially popular in the spring and summer.

Pass/Permit/Fees: It costs $5 for a single ride ticket or $6 for a ride on the Boardwalk Bullet. It also costs $20 to ride on the Boardwalk Beast. All-day ride passes are available for $24.99, but the Boardwalk Beast is not included.

Closest City or Town: League City

How to Get There: From downtown Houston, head down I-45 South and take Exit 24. Continue on the NASA Bypass and East NASA Parkway, then go south on Bayport Boulevard. Turn left on 6th Street and then take another left on Bradford Avenue.

GPS Coordinates: 29.54744 ° N, -95.02019 ° W

Did You Know? While the Boardwalk Bullet roller coaster is 3,200 feet long, it is extremely compact. It only takes up one acre of space.

Big Thicket National Preserve

Big Thicket National Preserve is about an hour and a half northeast of Houston and contains nine different ecosystems. There's something for everyone in this diverse, lush land.

This natural preserve protects and prioritizes wildlife, animals, and insects within its borders. There are miles of trails and waterways for folks to either hike or canoe. From the tall cypress trees to the low bayous, the range of ecosystems will leave you inspired and excited to spend a camping trip in this national park.

Best Time to Visit: Spring or fall

Pass/Permit/Fees: There are no passes or fees to enter.

Closest City or Town: Kountze

How to Get There: There isn't a main entrance to the preserve, but there is a visitor center. The best route is to follow I-10 East to Wallisville. Take exit 812 from I-10 East, then turn left onto TX-61 North. From there, turn right onto US-90 East and left onto TX-326 North/Old U.S. 90. Use the left two lanes to turn left onto US-287 North/US-69 North/S. Pine St. Turn right onto FM 420 East.

GPS coordinates: 30.458251° N, -94.387285° W

Did you know? The increase in infrastructure and industry is what eventually drove Big Thicket to become a national preserve in 1974.

Lake Fork

When we think of coasts and shores in Texas, we often think of the Gulf of Mexico. People tend to underestimate the natural beauty of the state's reservoirs and lakes. Down here, they say, "Life is better at the lake."

If you're searching for that, then travel 65 miles east of Dallas, where you'll find Lake Fork on Lake Fork Creek. Lake Fork is over 27,000 acres and offers over 300 miles of coastline! It's the perfect spot for vacationers to stop and enjoy fishing, boating, swimming, and other water activities, as well as hiking and biking along its scenic shores.

Best Time to Visit: It's beautiful all year, but the best time to visit Lake Fork is in the spring, fall, or summer.

Pass/Permit/Fees: It's free to visit Lake Fork, but depending on the activities you choose, you may need to pay a fee for entry.

Closest City or Town: Lake Fork

How to Get There: From Dallas: Get on I-20 East in Mesquite via E. Malloy Bridge Rd. Follow I-20 East, TX-34 North, and TX-276 East to FM 515 East/Lake Fork Drive in Emory. Follow FM 515 East and Co Rd 1970 to Peninsula Drive in Wood County.

GPS coordinates: 32.8311° N, -95.5830° W

Did you know? Lake Fork is known for its largemouth bass fishing. In fact, it currently holds the records for the top 34 largemouth bass caught in the state of Texas.

Little Elm Park

Little Elm Park is located along Lake Lewisville, northwest of Plano. It contains a beautiful, refreshing, and energizing beach. Equipped with a handful of beach volleyball nets, Little Elm Beach offers some of the largest open swimming locations for Texans and out-of-state visitors to enjoy during the hot summer months.

Along with its volleyball courts, the beach offers paddle-boarding, kayaking, swimming, and bike rentals from a nearby surf shop.

The park also has beachside dining at their Lakefront Grill, or you can always bring your own food and have a picnic with family and friends. The surrounding area has food and drink options for you to enjoy, and the summer offers lots of things to do for all ages.

Best Time to Visit: For swimming and water activities, summer is the best month to visit Little Elm Beach.

Pass/Permit/Fees: There is no fee for entrance, but you may have to pay for events and other activities along the beach.

Closest City or Town: Little Elm

How to Get There: Follow I-35 North to S. Interstate 35 South. Take exit 458.

GPS coordinates: 33.1587° N, -96.9484° W

Did you know? Little Elm Beach is located inside Little Elm Park.

Gorman Falls

Gorman Falls is two hours northwest of Austin. It's a beautiful state park that many Austinites and other locals love to visit. Gorman State Park is also home to Gorman Falls and Spicewood Springs.

This state park is a relaxing destination for those who want to cool off, fish, paddle, or boat along its waters. It also offers over 35 miles of hiking and bike trails for folks to explore. You can even go on a self-guided tour of the waterfalls, which is a three-mile roundtrip hike.

The park offers guests a more rugged camping experience, with sites that are meant for backwoods campers. There are some campsites that have water but no hookups.

Best Time to Visit: Spring or fall when the weather isn't too hot

Pass/Permit/Fees: Guests 13 years and older are $5. Children under 12 are free.

Closest City or Town: Lometa

How to Get There: Take I-35, US-183 North, Route 183A North, and US-183 North to W. North Ave in Lampasas. Take Farm to Market Road 580 to Gorman Road in San Saba County.

GPS coordinates: 31.022965° N, -98.442401° W

Did you know? Texas Parks and Wildlife purchased this park in 1984.

Capote Falls

Right outside of Marfa, way out in West Texas, Capote Falls is the state's biggest and proudest waterfall. It stands at an amazing 175 feet tall; everything is bigger here, after all. For a state that's known for its deserts, Texas has some beautiful waterfalls as well, and Capote Falls makes it to the top of the list.

Unfortunately, this waterfall is privately owned and can only be seen by air unless you know the owners, of course. Because of its lack of visitors, it's in pristine condition, and the surrounding habitat is preserved.

You may not be able to swim in Capote Falls but seeing its beauty from the air is a rare gift only a few get to enjoy.

Best Time to Visit: The best time to visit is unknown as it doesn't accept public guests.

Pass/Permit/Fees: There are no passes, permits, or fees.

Closest City or Town: Marfa

How to Get There: N/A

GPS coordinates: 30.2143° N, -104.5596° W

Did you know? The waterfall drains into the Rio Grande Rift and the Sierra Vieja, which flow towards the Rio Grande River.

Marfa Lights

The Marfa Lights are said to be the most continuous supernatural occurrence to happen in Texas. People travel from around the world to see this mysterious phenomenon. It's still unproven exactly what these lights are. Some people say they are paranormal activity, while other, more cynical people will say they're atmospheric reflections of cars and campfires at night.

Whether you're a believer in the supernatural or not, the Marfa Lights are sure to elicit a puzzling reaction. What exactly *are* they? Sometimes, they're red, and other times, they're blue or white. They appear any time of year and in any type of weather.

If you'd like to see the lights for yourself, travel nine miles west on Route US 90 and wait.

Best Time to Visit: Any time of year. However, it's best to travel to Marfa in the spring, fall, or winter when it's not so hot.

Pass/Permit/Fees: There are no passes or fees to see the Marfa Lights.

Closest City or Town: Marfa

How to Get There: The Marfa Lights Viewing Area is between Alpine and Marfa on US 90.

GPS coordinates: 30.27869° N, -103.88330° W

Did you know? There have been reports of the Marfa Lights since the 19th century, and their cause is still unknown.

Matagorda Bay Nature Park

Along Texas's Gulf Coast, there is a majestic and natural area filled with beauty, adventure, and refreshing water to escape the oppressive Texas heat. The Matagorda Bay Nature area spans 1,300 acres of marshes, beaches, and wetland areas. Matagorda Nature Park also has options for every type of camper. From the glamper to the rugged, backwoods type, there are options for everyone. The park has two airstream trailers that can be rented out with full amenities like air conditioning and running water. There is also an RV park and campsites for you to enjoy. At Matagorda Nature Park, you can enjoy a number of water activities, including swimming, boating, and fishing, as well as land activities like birdwatching, horseback riding, and mini-golf.

Best Time to Visit: Summer, but the park offers activities all year round

Pass/Permit/Fees: There are varying fees for entry based on age, lodging, and other factors.

Closest City or Town: Matagorda

How to Get There: Follow TX-71 to FM 1468 Hwy North in Matagorda County. Turn right onto TX-35 South. Continue on FM1468 to Wadsworth. Turn right onto TX-60 South, then left onto FM2031.

GPS coordinates: 28.60118° N, -95.97738° W

Did you know? Matagorda Bay Nature Park is part of the Lower Colorado River Authority (LCRA).

Schlitterbahn Waterpark

The Schlitterbahn Waterpark in New Braunfels is a fun place to visit during the summer months. The park contains dozens of exciting water rides and pools.

The park features the Master Blaster, a water coaster that runs over a thousand feet in length. You can also take a tube down the Hillside Chute, or you can go on one of the park's many waterslides. There's also a heated pool for adults with a swim-up bar. The park also features a few restaurants, including a pizza parlor and a burger bar. You'll also find shops throughout the park.

Best Time to Visit: Come to the waterpark on weekdays when possible, as the park can become crowded on weekends.

Pass/Permit/Fees: It costs $39.95 to enter the waterpark.

Closest City or Town: New Braunfels

How to Get There: From Austin, take I-35 South, then exit off Post Road in New Braunfels. Turn right on Gruene Road, then go left on Common Street. Turn right on Liberty Avenue. From San Antonio, take I-35 North and exit onto Schmidt Avenue, which eventually becomes West San Antonio Street. Turn left on Liberty Avenue to get to the park.

GPS Coordinates: 29.33372 ° N, -94.84584 ° W

Did You Know? The Schlitterbahn name comes from the German word for "slippery road." The name honors New Braunfels's German background.

Monahans Sandhills State Park

Monahans Sandhills State Park is like Texas's biggest sandbox. The sand in this western part of the state forms into dunes and valleys and is a one-of-a-kind desert environment. Locals and Texans call this place *an ocean of sand.*

About a half hour's drive from Odessa, this state park contains over 3,800 acres and spans both Ward and Winkler counties.

Take time to explore the wildlife havens, hike on the sand dunes, or even walk through the mini forest. At the Monahans Sandhills State Park, there is an ever-changing landscape for you to enjoy.

Best Time to Visit: Spring or fall. The cooler temperatures make visiting Monahans Sandhills State Park much more enjoyable.

Pass/Permit/Fees: Adults 13 years and older have an entrance fee of $4. Children under 12 are free.

Closest City or Town: Odessa

How to Get There: To reach the park, travel along Interstate 20 and exit at mile marker 86 to Park Road 41.

GPS coordinates: 31.6189° N, -102.8120° W

Did you know? There isn't any shade at Monahans Sandhills, so be careful with the sun's rays if you go during the day.

Lake Bob Sandlin State Park

In Texas's vastness, you're sure to find a variety of ecosystems, climates, and species of wildlife. Lake Bob Sandlin State Park is unique because it's where two of these ecosystems meet. While visiting this state park, you'll see giant trees to the east and the tall grasses of the Texas Plains to the west. East Texas is known for its swampland and lush greenery. Lake Bob Sandlin State Park has acres of forest along the lake's shoreline, where guests can fish, boat, hike, bike, and nature watch. Whoever thinks Texas doesn't show a change in the seasons is wrong. At Lake Bob Sandlin, autumn boasts beautiful fall foliage and is a must-see stop for anyone traveling in the area.

Best Time to Visit: Fall is the best time to view the foliage.

Pass/Permit/Fees: Adults 13 years or younger are $4. Children under 12 are free.

Closest City or Town: Pittsburgh

How to Get There: Lake Bob Sandlin State Park is approximately 12 miles southwest of Mount Pleasant. Take Interstate 30 to Highway 37 South at Mount Vernon and continue for 0.8 miles. Turn left onto Highway 21. The park entrance is 11.2 miles down.

GPS coordinates: 33.053955° N, -95.099155° W

Did you know? The Caddo people called East Texas home from the year 800 through 1860, which included the land in Lake Bob Sandlin State Park.

Port Aransas Beach

Known to locals and Texans alike as "Port A," Port Aransas is one of Texas's top summer destinations along the Gulf Coast. Home to popular attractions like Beachtoberfest, Art Fiesta Weekend, and the Harvest Moon Regatta, this beachy town is a hotspot for those wanting to enjoy some summertime fun in Texas.

Port Aransas consists of five miles of coastline along the 18-mile barrier island. Barrier Islands like Port A protect the islands from destructive hurricanes, waves, and other natural disasters.

If you're looking for a Texas hotspot to escape to for a summer vacation of family fun, Port Aransas is sure to have activities for everyone to enjoy.

Best Time to Visit: Port A is a popular Texas summer destination.

Pass/Permit/Fees: There are no fees to enter Port Aransas, but there may be fees for certain activities along its beaches.

Closest City or Town: Port Aransas

How to Get There: Take I-37 South to S. Padre Island Drive/Park Road 22 in Corpus Christi, then take TX-361 North to Port Aransas Beach Road in Port Aransas.

GPS coordinates: 27.8274° N, -97.0530° W

Did you know? The island of Port Aransas was first known as "Wild Horse Island" because of the wild horses the Spaniards brought to the area in the 1800s.

Magnolia Beach

Magnolia Beach sits along the Texas coastline. Unlike many beaches, this one offers hard sand, making it easy for cars, trucks, and RVs to drive and camp on the shoreline.

The beach stretches 1.5 miles along Matagorda Bay, which is about 20 minutes south of the small town of Port Lavaca. While this isn't your typical vacation beach, it does offer a peaceful getaway for avid campers and RVers to escape. There are beautiful views of water and sand.

However, quiet and picturesque comes at a cost. There aren't a lot of amenities in the surrounding town, so it's recommended to bring all of your essentials before parking on Magnolia Beach.

Best Time to Visit: Spring or summer. Summer if you'd like to go swimming!

Pass/Permit/Fees: There are no permits or fees to park your car at Magnolia Beach.

Closest City or Town: Port Lavaca

How to Get There: Take TX-130 South, US-183 South, and US-87 South to FM 2433 in Calhoun County. Take exit 223 toward TX-45 Toll/FM 1327/Creedmoor.

GPS coordinates: 28.5603° N, -96.5428° W

Did you know? Because the Colorado and Lavaca rivers flow through this beach, it is less salty than the Gulf of Mexico.

Island View Park

Island View Park is about an hour and a half north of Dallas/Fort Worth in Pottsboro. A sandy beach and summer attraction for North Texans, it's a refreshing day trip getaway for out of towners as well.

The beach offers sandy shores along Lake Texoma. Guests can enjoy summertime activities like swimming, kayaking, paddle-boarding, picnic areas, sunset evening boat rides, and a number of beach sports.

Pets are also welcome at Island View Park as long as they're on a leash. Shelters for gatherings and events can also be rented by the hour or day.

Best Time to Visit: For swimming and other water activities, summer is the best time. If you'd just like to enjoy the view or have a picnic, spring is also a great option!

Pass/Permit/Fees: $7 entrance fee per person. Kids under 7 are free.

Closest City or Town: Pottsboro

How to Get There: From the south: Take I-35 North towards US-75 North. Take Exit 70. From the north: Take I-35 South towards US-75 South. Take Exit 70.

GPS coordinates: 33.8595463°N, -96.6711079°W

Did you know? Lake Texoma is one of the largest reservoirs in the country. It separates Texas from Oklahoma.

Westcave Waterfalls

Westcave Waterfalls is about 45 minutes west of Austin. It's located near Hamilton Pool, which is equally beautiful. So, if you're traveling in this area, you must stop and see both.

Westcave Waterfalls is located in the Westcave Discovery Center, which prioritizes the preservation and protection of natural habitats and resources.

This center is all about conservation, collaboration, and educating its visitors to be more sustainable and environmentally-friendly citizens. Stopping by Westcave Waterfalls will be both an educational and inspiring adventure.

Best Time to Visit: Spring or summer, as this is when the area is lush with greenery and many native plants are in bloom.

Pass/Permit/Fees: $60 per household group.

Closest City or Town: Road Mountain

How to Get There: Take Highway 290 to Fitzhugh Road. Turn left on Hamilton Pool Road.

GPS coordinates: 30.339045° N, -98.140838° W

Did you know? You'll find a lot of native plants on this preserve, including the Texas persimmon, Ashe juniper, Texas live oak and dozens more.

Rockport Beach

Rockport Beach in Aransas County is located on the Gulf Coast. It stretches along Aransas Bay and is a popular tourist attraction for summer vacationers to the Texas shoreline.

If traveling to Rockport, stop at Rockport Beach Park for some daytime fun. The park features a saltwater pool, boat ramps, pavilions for small or larger gatherings, and plenty of swimming for all ages.

The beach is home to whooping cranes, which fly down to Aransas County in the wintertime. It's also a popular spot for birdwatching, fishing, and other outdoor summer activities.

Best Time to Visit: For swimming and water activities, it's best to visit in the summer. However, the beach is open to visitors year-round.

Pass/Permit/Fees: Parking fees are required.

Closest City or Town: Rockport

How to Get There: Take US-77 South to TX239 Ramp to Tivoli/Goliad, then turn left on TX-239 East. Keep right to continue on TX-35 South.

GPS coordinates: 28.0272° N, -97.0456° W

Did you know? Live oaks fill the town of Rockport. It's home to the state's famous live oak, named "The Big Tree."

Amazing Mirror Maze

The Amazing Mirror Maze in San Antonio is one of the most inviting and unique family attractions in the city. The site features multiple mazes that offer some unique scenes. The original Amazing Mirror Maze uses various mirrors angles to create unending hallways and unique lighting effects. You can wear 4D glasses while in the maze for a fun visual experience.

The complex also includes a funhouse mirror maze, a laser maze where you need to avoid as many lasers as possible, and a holographic maze that produces unique virtual environments. There are also six escape rooms in the Amazing Mirror Maze complex. Each room has a unique theme and various challenges.

Best Time to Visit: The maze complex is open year-round.

Pass/Permit/Fees: A single-day pass is $25.99. It may cost extra to reserve one of the escape rooms.

Closest City or Town: San Antonio

How to Get There: Take Exit 158 on I-35 to I-37 South. Take Exit 141A from the highway and turn right on E. Commerce Street. The maze complex is right on Alamo Plaza.

GPS Coordinates: 29.42515 ° N, -98.48724 ° W

Did You Know? The Infinity Maze uses specially designed mirrors and lights to create a layout that looks like it goes on forever.

GO RIO River Cruises

Take a ride down San Antonio's River Walk on a river cruise. GO RIO River Cruises start off at the eastern end of the River Walk near Commerce and Market Streets.

GO RIO offers 35-minute narrated cruises where you can learn about San Antonio's history and culture. You'll also learn about the distinct architecture surrounding the River Walk.

GO RIO also offers various specialty cruises throughout the year. These include a brunch cruise on Sundays and a cocktail cruise on Tuesdays. Other cruises include a horticultural tour cruise and private birthday cruises.

Best Time to Visit: The morning hours are the best time to visit, as the crowds will not be as strong.

Pass/Permit/Fees: A cruise costs $13.50 for adults, $10.50 for seniors, and $7.50 for kids.

Closest City or Town: San Antonio

How to Get There: Take the Commerce Street exit off of I-37 and go a few blocks to reach the GO RIO station. The station is across the street from the San Antonio Marriott River Walk.

GPS Coordinates: 29.42324 ° N, -98.48479 ° W

Did You Know? GO RIO offers cycle class cruises where you can pedal on a stationary bike while the cruise runs.

Gruene Historic District

The Gruene Historic District in New Braunfels is a neighborhood in the northern end of town near the Guadalupe River. The district features many 19th-century homes built by the German immigrants who first settled in the area. The district is home to various eateries and antique shops. The Gruene General Store has a full soda fountain and fudge shop. You can also sample one of more than fifty olive oils at the Gruene Olive Tasting Room. The Grapevine is popular among visitors, as it offers one of the most massive wine and beer selections in the state. You can also catch live music at the Gruene Hall, a dance hall built in 1878. It is Texas's oldest continuously operating dance hall.

Best Time to Visit: October is an ideal time, as the Texas Clay Festival occurs in Gruene during this month.

Pass/Permit/Fees: It's free to visit the district.

Closest City or Town: San Antonio

How to Get There: From San Antonio, take I-35 North to Exit 191. Turn left on FM 306, then turn left on Hunter Road. Take a right onto New Braunfels Street. From Austin, take I-35 South to Exit 195, turning right on Watson Lane West and then left on Hunter Road.

GPS Coordinates: 29.73872 ° N, -98.10395 ° W

Did You Know? The Gristmill River Restaurant and Bar was originally built as a cotton gin powered by the Guadalupe River.

Japanese Tea Garden

The Japanese Tea Garden is a quaint and peaceful space in Breckenridge Park in San Antonio. The garden is in an old limestone rock quarry and features many beautiful sites that provide an oasis away from the city.

You'll enter a Japanese Torii gate to reach the garden. Throughout the venue, a cement kiln, pagodas, houses, and a small amphitheater break up the lush growth.

Take a stroll down the relaxing series of walkways surrounding several artificial ponds. You will notice a few small islands with plants throughout the garden. Many of the bridges going over the water are covered in vines and other Asian plants.

Best Time to Visit: The park is open year-round, but it is especially peaceful in the morning.

Pass/Permit/Fees: It is free to visit the garden.

Closest City or Town: San Antonio

How to Get There: From the center of San Antonio, take I-37 North to US 281 North. Exit onto Mulberry Avenue, then go north on St. Mary's Street. The garden is next to the San Antonio Zoo.

GPS Coordinates: 29.46113 ° N, -98.47700 ° W

Did You Know? The venue has a teahouse that also serves small meals.

Medina River

The Medina River lies on the south side of San Antonio. A quaint river that flows through a natural area, it has been attracting visitors and campers since its inception.

The Medina River Natural Area is a 511-acre property with seven miles of trails to hike and take a leisurely walk. During the spring, its banks are covered in beautiful Texas wildflowers. The area has a remarkable blend of pecan and cypress trees with blooming cactus, making it a quintessential stop for folks visiting the San Antonio area.

There are camping options as well. This natural area has a covered pavilion for small gatherings and camping amenities that can be rented by the hour.

Best Time to Visit: Year-round. However, it's always best to avoid the hot Texas heat in the summer months.

Pass/Permit/Fees: The only fees are for camping and renting the pavilion. These can vary.

Closest City or Town: San Antonio

How to Get There: From I-35, take exit 149 toward TX-422 Spur/TX-16/Poteet/Palo Alto Road. The Medina River Natural Area is located at 15890 Highway 16 South.

GPS coordinates: 29.263801° N, -98.578637° W

Did you know? The Medina River is home to the green kingfisher and painted bunting.

Mission San Jose

The Mission San Jose was built in 1720 on the southern end of San Antonio. The venue is a UNESCO World Heritage site that was refurbished in the 1930s by the Works Projects Administration.

The church offers many sites you can visit, including an old granary, the soldiers' quarters, and a grist mill. The mission also hosts a church that continues to operate today, which caters to weddings and other special religious events.

You can learn about the history of the mission while here. It was originally built by Spanish missionaries to promote the Christian faith.

Best Time to Visit: You can visit the mission throughout the week. Sunday masses are offered in English at 9 a.m. and in Spanish at noon.

Pass/Permit/Fees: It is free to visit the mission.

Closest City or Town: San Antonio

How to Get There: The mission is about five miles south of downtown San Antonio. Take S. St. Mary's Street and Roosevelt Avenue to reach the mission.

GPS Coordinates: 29.36239 ° N, -98.47971 ° W

Did You Know? Most of the border walls surrounding the mission feature the original limestone materials used in construction in 1720.

The Natural Bridge Caverns

The Natural Bridge Caverns are the largest caverns in the entire state of Texas, which makes this a top natural attraction. Geologists theorize that Texas was once underwater, so the caverns are preserved with different layers of limestone, sedimentary rock, and fossils.

There are a number of different ways to see the caverns, from discovery tours to hidden passage tours. There are countless places to explore. Guided tours of the caves allow for more in-depth knowledge and learning about the caverns' rich prehistoric history from a professional.

Best Time to Visit: Year-round

Pass/Permit/Fees: Fees depend on tour selection and the age of the visitor.

Closest City or Town: San Antonio

How to Get There: Head north on I-35 and take Exit 175. Turn left (west) on Natural Bridge Caverns Road/F.M. 3009.

GPS coordinates: 29.6924° N, -98.3427° W

Did you know? The caverns were formed from thousands of years of river water running through limestone.

San Antonio Botanical Garden

The San Antonio Botanical Garden provides a quaint and peaceful oasis in the heart of the city with nearly forty acres of gardens. The garden has many native plants and a few themed gardens. These include an herb garden, a Biblical garden, and a Japanese garden inspired by the Suizenji Park garden in Kyoto.

The Lucille Halsell Conservatory maintains plants from around the world in an indoor environment. There are five greenhouses here, with each supporting a different climate. You'll find separate sections dedicated to tropical plants, carnivorous plants, and succulents.

Best Time to Visit: The garden is open year-round, but the spring season is the best time to visit. The garden is in full bloom during the spring.

Pass/Permit/Fees: Adults can enter the garden for $15. Kids 13 and under cost $12.

Closest City or Town: San Antonio

How to Get There: Take I-37 North and US-281 North to reach the garden from the center of San Antonio. Travel east on Hildebrand Avenue, turning right on New Braunfels Avenue.

GPS Coordinates: 29.45853 ° N, -98.45795 ° W

Did You Know? The Garden for the Blind section of the complex features many plants with distinctive textures and scents, providing a unique experience for the visually impaired.

San Antonio Missions National Historical Park

Many of the oldest sites in San Antonio are missions established by the Catholic Church to spread their faith to natives. The San Antonio Missions National Historical Park is home to the San Jose Mission. Much of the original 1720 structure remains intact and is on display for all to see.

The park spreads over nearly a thousand acres of land. The area includes various walking paths that will take you throughout the entire landscape. You'll also find the Ethel Wilson Harris House at the northern end of the park. The house features a Modern Movement design from Robert Harris.

Best Time to Visit: The park is open throughout the year.

Pass/Permit/Fees: It is free to visit the park area.

Closest City or Town: San Antonio

How to Get There: The park is south of downtown San Antonio. Go south on I-37, then take Exit 138C to Fair Avenue. Turn left on S. Hackberry, then go right on E. Southcross. Turn left on Roosevelt Avenue, and you'll find the park on the left.

GPS Coordinates: 29.36061 ° N, -98.47947 ° W

Did You Know? The church continues to host regular masses throughout the year.

San Antonio's River Walk

Follow the San Antonio River Walk over 15 miles alongside the San Antonio River. Five miles of the path run right through the heart of the city.

The River Walk features various dining and shopping outlets, and it offers boat rides in many places. You'll pass by several noteworthy sites while on the River Walk, including St. Mary's Church, the Torch of Friendship, and the International Center.

The River Walk also hosts many museums, including the Buckhorn Saloon and Museum, the Briscoe Western Art Museum, and a Ripley's Believe It or Not location.

Best Time to Visit: The River Walk is open all year round. The morning hours are especially great, as the River Walk can get busy at night.

Pass/Permit/Fees: It is free to visit the River Walk, although some nearby attractions cost money to visit.

Closest City or Town: San Antonio

How to Get There: You can reach the River Walk from I-37 on Exit 141. The most prominent parts of the River Walk are around E. Commerce Street.

GPS Coordinates: 29.42451 ° N, -98.48826 ° W

Did You Know? There are plenty of events at the River Walk throughout the year. *Rio Magazine* will help you learn about the latest developments here before you visit.

SeaWorld San Antonio

SeaWorld San Antonio introduces guests to the amazing aquatic world with up-close and personal entertainment. The amusement park is home to various unique sea mammals, including five killer whales and ten beluga whales. You'll also find bottlenose dolphins, sea lions, and otters at the park. SeaWorld San Antonio houses more than 200 birds at its Penguin House.

The amusement park section of SeaWorld San Antonio provides many thrill rides, including the Texas Stingray and Steel Eel roller coasters.

Best Time to Visit: The park is open during the spring and summer seasons. The park is not as busy during the weekdays.

Pass/Permit/Fees: It costs $113.99 for a ticket to the park, although you can spend $89.99 if you reserve a ticket for a specific day.

Closest City or Town: San Antonio

How to Get There: The park is on the western end of San Antonio. Take the TX-151 West exit from I-410, then take the route up to Westover Hills Boulevard. Turn left, and you'll see the entrance to Sea World.

GPS Coordinates: 29.46316 ° N, -98.70204 ° W

Did You Know? The park features a Sesame Street–themed amusement area for kids. Younger kids will enjoy rides like Super Grover's Box Car Derby and Abby Cadabby's Rockin' Wave.

The Alamo

The Alamo may be the most iconic attraction in all of Texas. The old Spanish mission is available for tours. The Alamo was critical to the Texas Revolution and remains an essential symbol of the state. You'll learn about its immense value while you visit the site in San Antonio. You can take a tour of the Alamo and watch various demonstrations of military equipment and other items used in the Alamo during the siege on the building in 1836. The battleground includes an authentic full-size cannon. The museum at the Alamo includes many artifacts showing the building's story. You'll learn about the role of the Alamo during the Texas Revolution and how it was critical to the state's history.

Best Time to Visit: The Alamo is open year-round, but spring is a great time to visit as the trees around the area are in bloom.

Pass/Permit/Fees: The Alamo is free to visit, but a reservation is required.

Closest City or Town: San Antonio

How to Get There: The Alamo is on the Alamo Plaza near E. Houston Street in downtown San Antonio. It is also a few blocks east of the River Walk and north of the Rivercenter shopping mall.

GPS Coordinates: 29.42611 ° N, -98.48620 ° W

Did You Know? The Alamo building was originally built as a mission in 1718.

Caverns of Sonora

The Caverns of Sonora feature some of the most beautiful cave formations around. These include limestone shapes that formed over millions of years. You'll notice many helictites around the caverns. Helictites are unique mineral growths that change from the vertical to horizontal axis many times as they form, producing what looks like a zero-gravity body.

The caverns also feature many flowstone developments. These form when water flows down the walls of the cave, producing a wavy multi-tone look that has the nickname "cave bacon." There are around two miles of trail, although seven miles have been explored over the years. A guided tour operator will lead you throughout the many unique sites around the caverns.

Best Time to Visit: The climate is temperate in the caverns throughout the year, so you could visit at any time you wish.

Pass/Permit/Fees: It costs $20 to enter the caverns.

Closest City or Town: Sonora

How to Get There: Take I-10 West from San Antonio or Austin, or I-10 East from El Paso. Take Exit 392 and follow Caverns Road to the south.

GPS Coordinates: 30.55976 ° N, -100.81214 ° W

Did You Know? The caverns weren't officially discovered until the early twentieth century. It also wasn't explored further until the 1950s.

Krause Springs

The small town of Spicewood is home to a beautiful, quiet, and refreshing summer escape. This well-known, locally owned area is found in the beautiful Texas Hill Country. It offers guests a variety of summertime swimming options in a fresh, spring-fed pool or natural swimming hole. Enjoy camping, swimming, picnicking, and other outdoor activities at Krause Springs. At the top of the property is a manmade pool that, due to the springs, is always at a cool, refreshing temperature. Hike down just a bit, and you'll find a natural swimming hole with a limestone beach to sunbathe and relax. Krause Springs is also known for its high rope swing; only the most adventurous dare to swing and plunge into the cold depths of the springs.

Best Time to Visit: For swimming, the best time to visit is summer. If you'd like to hike or camp, spring is also a beautiful time to visit.

Pass/Permit/Fees: Fees vary based on day, age, group, and camping selections.

Closest City or Town: Spicewood

How to Get There: From Austin, take Texas Highway 71 West. Cross the Pedernales River and drive seven more miles. Turn right on Spur 191, then right again on County Road 404. The gates for Krause Springs are on the left.

GPS coordinates: 30.4777° N, -98.1517° W

Did you know? There are a total of 32 natural springs on the property.

George Ranch Historical Park

You will find the George Ranch Historical Park southwest of Houston. The full-sized ranch was founded in 1824.

The park shows the evolution of Texas from the formation of the park through the 20th century. There is a log cabin and a few outdoor kitchens on the stock farm. There's also an 1890s Victorian house with a blacksmith shop and a sharecropping farm.

A cattle complex located on the site allows guests to watch cowboys rope and sort longhorn cattle. A half-mile trail wraps around Dry Creek, a body of water in the middle of the historical park. You'll see many old prairie surroundings here.

Best Time to Visit: The park features historical reenactments during the spring season.

Pass/Permit/Fees: It costs $15 for adults to enter and $10 for kids.

Closest City or Town: Sugar Land

How to Get There: From Houston, go south on I-69 and take Exit 105 to Crabb River Road. Keep going south onto FM 762.

GPS Coordinates: 29.49978 ° N, -95.68214 ° W

Did You Know? The park is on the western end of Smithers Lake, one of the largest lakes in the Houston area.

Surfside Beach

Known to locals simply as "Surfside," this Texas beach town offers visitors a charming, quiet place to escape in the summer. This beach is located on Follet's Island along the Gulf of Mexico.

This tiny beach town is a perfect contrast to popular beaches like Port A or South Padre. If you're looking for a more low-key, relaxing vibe, this is your dream destination. In 2010, the census recorded the population of this small town as just 482 people.

Best Time to Visit: For water activities, it's best to visit Surfside in the summer, but the town is beautiful and quaint all year round.

Pass/Permit/Fees: There are no fees to enter Surfside Beach.

Closest City or Town: Surfside Beach

How to Get There: Take I-10 to Exit 699 toward FM102/Eagle Lake. Follow FM102 South to E. Main Street in Eagle Lake. Follow US-90 ALT East to Beasley Road/Farm-To-Market Road 1875/FM 1875 Road in Fort Bend County. Continue on Farm-To-Market Rd 1875, then take FM 360 Road to TX-36 South in Needville. Follow TX-36 South, TX-35 North, and State Highway 288 South to TX-332 East in Lake Jackson. Take the TX-332 East exit from State Highway 288 South.

GPS coordinates: 28.95272° N, -95.28523° W

Did you know? Former congressman Ron Paul owns a beach home in Surfside.

Big Bend National Park

Big Bend National Park is one of the most beautiful places to travel to in Texas. During the day, the red Chisos Mountains sprawl high and tall against a beautiful blue sky. At night, the stars illuminate a history and culture that is both sacred and simple. Big Bend sits along the Rio Grande River and shares a border with Mexico to its south. The park is home to the entire Chisos Mountain Range and a large portion of the Chihuahuan Desert.

Best Time to Visit: It's best to plan a trip to Big Bend National Park, either in the milder spring or fall weather. Winter and summer temperatures tend to be extreme and pose challenges for campers and visitors.

Pass/Permit/Fees: No reservation is required. Park visitors are required to purchase a recreational pass. Fees vary depending on the vehicle, group size and desired camping accommodations.

Closest City or Town: Terlingua

How to Get There: The distance between towns is significant. Be sure to have enough gas, oil, and food to make the trip.

TX 118 from Alpine to Study Butte
FM 170 from Presidio to Study Butte

GPS coordinates: 29.2498° N, -103.2502° W

Did you know? Big Bend National Park is home to over 450 species of birds.

Cattails Falls

Surprisingly, there is a moderately popular hiking spot near Big Bend National Park that ends in a cascading oasis. What makes its relative secrecy so special is the beautiful paradise at the end of the hike: Cattails Falls.

The hike is only about 1.5 miles into the canyon. It's not recommended to take these hikes in the summer, as the heat can be aggressive and dangerous for even the most experienced hikers. Sometimes, drought years offer a less-than-exciting end. So, be sure that you hike here when the region has seen a decent amount of rainfall.

Once you escape the desert and enter into more of the lush greenery, be on the lookout for wild black bears!

Best Time to Visit: Spring or summer

Pass/Permit/Fees: Cattails Falls is located in Big Bend National Park, so it is subject to their passes and fees.

Closest City or Town: Terlingua

How to Get There: Head south on Ross Maxwell Scenic Drive in Big Bend. After mile marker 3, look for a small opening beyond the Sam Nail Ranch overlook. It's easy to miss, so be on the lookout!

GPS coordinates: 29.2731° N, -103.3355° W

Did you know? Only the most seasoned Big Bend hikers travel to Cattails Falls every year.

Santa Elena Canyons

Few sites along the Rio Grande are as beautiful as the Santa Elena Canyons. Located in the western end of the Big Bend National Park, the canyons feature some of the tallest cliffs along the Rio Grande, with several rising to 1,500 feet high.

You'll find many rapids throughout the canyons, including those that enter Terlingua Creek. Paddle upstream into Santa Elena from the trailhead and then downstream on the way back.

Best Time to Visit: Visit during the fall or winter, as summer temperatures here can be dangerously high.

Pass/Permit/Fees: It's free to enter the canyons, but you will require a backcountry permit for an overnight river trip.

Closest City or Town: Terlingua

How to Get There: From Terlingua, go east on FM 170 and then south on TX-118. Go east on Panther Junction Road and then take a right on the Ross Maxwell Scenic Drive. The road eventually becomes the Santa Elena Canyon Road. It takes about 48 miles to travel from Terlingua to the canyon by car.

GPS Coordinates: 29.16610 ° N, -103.61219 ° W

Did You Know? You won't experience much of a current paddling upstream if the water levels are low.

Lost Maples State Natural Area

Located just two hours northwest of San Antonio, Lost Maples State Natural Area is known for its fall foliage, but it boasts natural beauty all year round.

This natural area highlights that Texas does actually change with the four seasons. Lost Maples is home to bigtooth maple trees that are known for turning all shades of red, orange, and yellow during the autumn season.

There are miles of hiking trails, stargazing opportunities, and plenty of camping grounds for families and friends to enjoy throughout the year.

Best Time to Visit: The fall is the most popular time, but there are activities open all year round.

Pass/Permit/Fees: Fees depend on visitors' ages and group information.

Closest City or Town: Vanderpool

How to Get There: The park is located five miles north of Vanderpool on Ranch Road 187.

GPS coordinates: 29.8076° N, -99.5706° W

Did you know? Lost Maples measures a three on the Bortle Dark-Sky Scale, which means there's enough darkness for viewing "celestial objects" like stars.

Cameron Park Zoo

The Cameron Park Zoo is on the southern shore of the Brazos River in Waco. The zoo features 52 acres of land and more than 300 species of animals. Located at the southern end of Cameron Park, it offers various habitats allowing a view of some of the world's most intriguing animals.

Some of the animals you'll find here include elephants, giraffes, jaguars, tigers, and orangutans. Allow your kids to cool off in a small splash zone and play area designed just for them. The Brazos River Country section of the zoo also has a 50,000-gallon aquarium highlighting many saltwater mammals.

Best Time to Visit: The zoo is open year-round.

Pass/Permit/Fees: Admission is $12.50 for adults, $11.50 for seniors, and $9.50 for kids.

Closest City or Town: Waco

How to Get There: From Dallas, go south on I-35 East and then take Exit 335C to downtown Waco. Go right on Martin Luther King Jr. Boulevard and cross the river at Franklin Avenue. Keep going northwest on University Parks Drive. From Austin, go north on I-35 and take Exit 334A. Go north on 17th Street and then right on US-84 and left on 4th Street.

GPS Coordinates: 31.571 ° N, -97.14466 ° W

Did You Know? Listen for the White-Handed Gibbons, whose calls can be heard from about half a mile away.

Dr Pepper Museum

The Dr Pepper Museum is in the heart of downtown Waco, where the soft drink was first bottled in the 1880s. The museum is inside a bottling plant that was built in 1906. The tour highlights the history of Dr Pepper, from its origins in Waco to how it has become one of the world's top sodas. You'll see many signs and artifacts relating to Dr Pepper's history and how the drink became popular.

The museum also offers information on many other drinks made by the Keurig Dr Pepper group. These include RC Cola, 7-Up, IBC Root Beer, and Big Red. There's a soda fountain on site that sells Dr Pepper floats and ice cream.

Best Time to Visit: The museum is open late during the summer months.

Pass/Permit/Fees: It costs $10 for adults and $6 for kids to visit the museum. It costs extra to participate in one of the special events here.

Closest City or Town: Waco

How to Get There: From Dallas, go south on I-35 and take Exit 335B. Turn right on E. 5th Street to reach the museum.

GPS Coordinates: 31.55476 ° N, -97.12914 ° W

Did You Know? You can try various Dr Pepper sodas from around the world at the museum's Taste-a-Soda attraction.

Waco Mammoth National Monument

Waco Mammoth National Monument sits along the Bosque River in North Texas and has over 100 acres of woodland. It's known for the mammoth fossils found in the park in the 1970s. Thousands of years ago, during the Ice Age, this region was home to the massive Columbian mammoth. This national monument is covered in Texas's very own oak, cedar, and mesquite trees. It also offers hiking and camping opportunities along with its rich history.

Best Time to Visit: Spring or fall

Pass/Permit/Fees: Fees vary based on age and occupation. There are discounts for military members, educators, students, and children.

Closest City or Town: Waco

How to Get There: From the north: Take Exit 339 off I-35 North. Lake Shore Drive will be on your right. Turn right onto Steinbeck Bend Drive and continue for another 1.5 miles until you reach the monument.

From the south: Take exit 335C off I-35 South. Make a left at Martin Luther King, Jr. Blvd. Continue on Steinbeck Bend Drive, and you'll see the monument in 1.5 miles.

GPS coordinates: 31.6067° N, -97.1758° W

Did you know? 16 Columbian mammoth fossils were found here from 1978 to 1990.

Jacob's Well

Jacob's Well is a sight to see. Its depth is both beautiful and a bit intimidating. While it's only 13 feet wide, the well is over 160 feet deep, making it extremely dangerous for deep-water diving. Dangling your feet from the edge of the well and looking down can feel like you're peering into the depths of the Earth through the clear blue water.

It's a summertime swimming favorite in the Texas Hill Country, though swimming is not permitted during certain times of year for water restoration purposes. There are many hiking trails for family and friends around the swimming hole as well. Dogs are not allowed.

Best Time to Visit: If you'd like to swim, make reservations for after April 30th. Springtime is best for hiking and sightseeing, while summer is best for swimming in the well.

Pass/Permit/Fees: Reservations are required for swimming but not visiting.

Closest City or Town: Wimberley

How to Get There: Jacob's Well Natural Area is located approximately 10 minutes from the city of Wimberley. The entrance to Jacob's Well Natural Area is located at 1699 Mount Sharp Road, Wimberley, TX 78676.

GPS coordinates: 30.0344° N, -98.1261° W

Did you know? Jacob's Well is the second-largest fully submerged cave in Texas.

Boykin Springs

There's another gem in East Texas that folks ought to see. Boykin Springs Recreation Area sits on Boykin Springs Lake within Angelina National Forest. This spot offers something for everyone. At Boykin Springs, you can camp, hike, bike, fish, picnic, or just relax in nature.

The recreation area also has a pavilion and picnic area that can accommodate a reservation of up to 74 people for a larger gathering.

Although there are no water hookups for campers, there are hot showers and running water for you to enjoy. Boykin Springs is a great trip for the rugged camper or day-tripper.

Best Time to Visit: Spring or fall

Pass/Permit/Fees: The park is free to enter, but there are fees for camping and renting the picnic area.

Closest City or Town: Zavalla

How to Get There: From Zavalla, travel east on Highway 63 for 10 miles. Turn right on Forest Service Road 313 and continue for two miles to the campground.

GPS coordinates: 31.06161940° N, -94.27461500° W

Did you know? Archeologists predict that humans have inhabited this land for 8,000 years.

Proper Planning

With this guide, you are well on your way to properly planning a marvelous adventure. When you plan your travels, you should become familiar with the area, save any maps to your phone for access without internet, and bring plenty of water—especially during the summer months. Depending on the adventure you choose, you will also want to bring snacks and even a lunch. For younger children, you should do your research and find destinations that best suits your family's needs. Additionally, you should also plan when to get gas, local lodgings and where to get food after you're finished. We've done our best to group these destinations based on nearby towns and cities to help make planning easier.

Dangerous Wildlife

There are several dangerous animals and insects you may encounter while hiking. With a good dose of caution and awareness, you can explore safely. Here is what you can do to keep yourself and your loved ones safe from dangerous flora and fauna while exploring:

- Keep to the established trails.
- Do not look under rocks, leaves, or sticks.
- Keep hands and feet out of small crawl spaces, bushes, covered areas, or crevices.
- Wear long sleeves and pants to keep arms and legs protected.
- Keep your distance should you encounter any dangerous wildlife or plants.

Limited Cell Service

Do not rely on cell service for navigation or emergencies. Always have a map with you and let someone know where you are and for how long you intend to be gone, just in case.

First Aid Information

Always travel with a first aid kit with you in case of emergencies.
Here are items to be certain to include in your primary first aid kit:
- Nitrile gloves
- Blister care products
- Band-aids - multiple sizes and waterproof type
- Ace wrap and athletic tape
- Alcohol wipes and antibiotic ointment
- Irrigation syringe
- Tweezers, nail clippers, trauma shears, safety pins
- Small Ziplock bags containing contaminated trash

It is recommended to also keep a secondary first aid kit, especially when hiking, for more serious injuries or medical emergencies. Items in this should include:
- Blood clotting sponges
- Sterile gauze pads
- Trauma pads
- Second-skin/burn treatment
- Triangular bandages/sling
- Butterfly strips
- Tincture of benzoin
- Medications (ibuprofen, acetaminophen, antihistamine, aspirin, etc.)

- Thermometer
- CPR mask
- Wilderness medicine handbook
- Antivenin

There is so much more to explore, but this is a great start.

For information on all national parks, visit: www.nps.gov.

This site will give you information on up-to-date entrance fees and how to purchase a park pass for unlimited access to national and state parks. These sites will also introduce you to all of the trails of each park.

Always check before you travel to destinations to make sure there are no closures. Some hikes close when there is heavy rain or snow in the area, and other parks close parts of their land for the migration of wildlife. Attractions may change their hours or temporarily shut down for various reasons. Check the websites for the most up-to-date information.